FRANCIS FRITH'S

# COLLECTED MEMORIES OF SOUTH WALES

THE FRANCIS FRITH COLLECTION

www.francisfrith.com

Collected Memories of

# South Wales

## West, South & Mid Glamorgan and Gwent

Inspired by The Francis Frith Collection®

THE FRANCIS FRITH COLLECTION

www.francisfrith.com

First published in the United Kingdom in 2013
by The Francis Frith Collection®

Paperback edition 2013 ISBN 978-1-84589-746-8



British Library Cataloguing in Publication Data

Collected Memories of South Wales - West, South & Mid Glamorgan and Gwent

The Francis Frith Collection®
6 Oakley Business Park, Wylye Road,
Dinton, Wiltshire SP3 5EU
Tel: +44 (0) 1722 716 376
Email: info@francisfrith.co.uk

www.francisfrith.com

Printed and bound in Great Britain
Contains material sourced from responsibly managed forests

*Front Cover:* TON PENTRE, Church Road c1965 T191001t
*Frontispiece:* MERTHYR TYDFIL, Upper High Street c1955 M118012t

***Every attempt has been made to contact copyright holders of illustrative material. We will be happy to give full acknowledgement in future editions for any items not credited. Any information should be directed to The Francis Frith Collection.***

*The colour-tinting in this book is for illustrative purposes only, and is not intended to be historically accurate*

***AS WITH ANY HISTORICAL DATABASE, THE FRANCIS FRITH ARCHIVE IS CONSTANTLY BEING CORRECTED AND IMPROVED, AND THE PUBLISHERS WOULD WELCOME INFORMATION ON OMISSIONS OR INACCURACIES***

# Collected Memories of South Wales – A Dedication

**This book has been compiled from a selection of the thousands of personal memories added by visitors to the Frith website and could not have happened without these contributions. We are very grateful to everyone who has taken the time to share their memories in this way. The combination of all these personal stories provides a wonderful insight into British life and this book is therefore dedicated to everyone who has taken the time to participate in the Frith Memories project.**

Each memory is personal to the writer yet the pictures painted are part of a shared inheritance, reminders of a life that so many people still cherish in their memories. For others, these memories will provide an insight into a way of life that has now vanished.

In the current uncertain times it is comforting to find so many stories full of human warmth which bring back happy memories of "the good old days". We hope that everyone reading this book will find stories that amuse and fascinate whilst at the same time be reminded of why we feel affection for Britain and what makes us all British.

Francis Frith always expressed the wish that his photographs be made available to as wide an audience as possible and so it is particularly pleasing to me that by creating the Frith website we have been able to make this nationally important photographic record of Britain available to a worldwide audience. Now, by providing the Share Your Memories feature on the website we are delighted to provide an opportunity for members of the public to record their own stories and to see them published (both on the website and perhaps in our books), ensuring that they are shared and not lost or forgotten.

We hope that you too will be motivated to visit our website and add your own memories to this growing treasure trove – helping us to make it an even more comprehensive record of the changes that have taken place in Britain in the last 100 years and a resource that will be valued by generations to come.

John M Buck
Managing Director

www.francisfrith.com

ABERTILLERY, Church Street c1955 A279001

# Contents

## Memories of the war years 1939-1945 in Newport

Little did I realise that I would be involved in the army when war broke out in 1939. I was attending Hatherleigh Central School in Newport at the time, and as a young lad did not really understand what the fuss was all about when it was announced that we had declared war on Germany, but I was soon to find out. It affected my education a great deal, because soon after war was declared the announcement was made by the authorities that only half of the schoolchildren would be in school at one time, in case a bomb was dropped. Half the schoolchildren went in the mornings and the other half went in the afternoons. If the sirens were sounded during the time we were in school, we had already rehearsed to evacuate the school to be boarded with families in the Christchurch /Gibbs Road area. There was no panicking, just an orderly march to our allocated address.

Unfortunately for me I did not complete my education. When I reached the age of fourteen, halfway through my third year at Hatherleigh, I was released for a job as a junior on the Great Western Railway in The District Goods Manager's Office, in High Street.

How well I remember the air-raid sirens going off during the war and everyone rushing to the air-raid shelters, sitting in the cold damp Anderson shelters listening to the German bombers passing overhead. The ack-ack guns situated around the town followed the searchlights scanning the sky for the enemy aircraft, and when the plane was spotted they opened fire with a salvo of shells which made a tremendous noise. This happened on many occasions, the planes were on their way to drop bombs elsewhere up country. After many sleepless nights and having to go to work the next morning, I decided that enough was enough and I would stay in bed whatever happened – until the night that Newport was about to get its share of the bombings. A land mine was dropped in Eveswell Street, which was a mile from where I lived. The blast from this was felt all over the town and this certainly did the trick of getting me out of bed, I think I would have broken all records at the time to get from bed to shelter. There were many broken windows in the area and damaged buildings surrounding Eveswell, but many houses were destroyed and lives lost where the land mine dropped. They were obviously aiming for the railway sidings, and the ammunitions factory nearby. As I passed the top of the street on my way to work the next morning the rescue services were still busy carrying out their duties. Despite all the sad events during this time, life carried on as normal. *John Beal* 129091

## I remember when the land mine dropped on Eveswell Street in Newport...

My father, John, was a doctor at his surgery/house on Corporation Road in Newport, and I and my brother John plus our mother and father were in the shelter when the mine was dropped on Eveswell Street during the war. I remember a discussion later about loss of panel patients in that street – our mother kept the books! I well remember the troops camping on the rugby pitch prior to D-Day. I went out one morning and all the troops were gone. It took me many years to realise they must have gone south to the ports just prior to D-Day. Before that, we kids were wonderfully entertained by 'shows' on the pitch particularly the Indian mounted troops doing their peg dancing. *Michael Savage* 398781

NEWPORT, The Docks, South Quay c1955 N25179

## This photograph brought back memories of wartime Newport...

I started an apprenticeship as a joiner in the Mountstuart ship-repairing dry docks and a lot of my time was spent on ships at the Alexander Dock. The Frith photograph of the South Quay brought back a lot of memories from the war period, of the installation of gun positions and the accommodation for the marine gunners on merchant vessels, the various preparations for vessels taking cargo and troops to North Africa, Malta and even Murmansk and, of course, eventually to Normandy. It was awe-inspiring in the latter part of the war watching the almost daily arrival of American Liberty Ships heavily loaded with deck cargo and other innovated ships for tanks and heavy vehicle loaded with a roll on, roll off technique. A very interesting and exciting time for an apprentice.

*Ernie Cann 328681*

## How we lived at Pontnewydd during the war

I lived at number 36 Commercial Street at Pontnewydd from 1936 for 11 years and saw the changes that the Second World War brought to our village. I remember the milkman and his horse-drawn cart and Mam asking for a gill (quarter pint) as she searched her purse for the coin to pay for it. Someone would always rush out to collect the horse droppings for use on their garden. I recall the blackouts and the sound of enemy aircraft overhead as they followed the mountain range from Blaenavon to Twyn Barllwm, their dropping point for the bombs aimed at Newport Docks. Then there was the arrival of the Yanks based at Llantarnam, and rides in jeeps to the Mountain Air pub when soldiers took our neighbour's daughters out for runs. *Lance Ford 28411*

## Life during the war at Glyn Hall, Mamhilad

We moved to Glyn Hall about 1942; my father and, later, my mother worked at the ROF Glascoed (a Government-owned Royal Ordnance Factory). I doubt that there would be any external photos as this was an extremely hush-hush site. It was built to accommodate managers and key-workers, and was a self-contained unit.

Our furniture (utility) was Government issue, the wooden, springless settee had two upholstered orange cushions. The canteen provided all our food, which seemed to consist of nothing but macaroni and lentils. I was fortunately on a special diet. On her day off my mother would cook on an electric ring, the stack of saucepans slowly rising throughout the day, the meat was probably rabbit!

There was a theatre for films, pantomimes and dances. We would sneak in to watch films through the emergency doors, thinking no-one would notice us! There was also a very small hospital with a casualty unit. I think there were only four beds in the ward, which was watched over by a nurse, through a window from the nurse's station.

The nursery school was equipped in a very child-friendly way, with low level toilets, hand basins and camp beds for our afternoon sleep. We were taught to use toothbrushes and wash our hands after using the indoor toilets. The walls were decorated with phonic alphabet pictures which helped me to read before I was four years old, although 'th' was a challenge. Mamhilad School was outside Glyn Hall and very different; coats, wet or dry, were hung in the vestibule and there was only a stove to heat the two classrooms. We were allowed to play in the orchard in front of the schoolhouse. On the return journey home we picked rose-hips as our contribution to the war effort. I don't know where they were sent for processing.

As the war was coming to an end American and Polish soldiers were billeted in or near Glyn Hall, and, as a four-year old child, I felt obliged to invite them home. Heaven only knows what they expected, but I knew that my parents would treat them with kindness and generosity. Once it was clear that Glyn Hall had served its purpose, new homes were planned for the families who had settled there. By August 1945 many families had moved into the prefabs in New Inn. I can remember VJ fireworks celebrations.

I believe that Glyn Hall has a unique history, which should be preserved. When we return home and speak to Pontypool people of our age, no-one, except those who lived in Glyn Hall, seems to know anything about it.

*Diana Lewis 104271*

# My time during the war at Tirphil

Whilst born in New Tredegar, I spent a great part of my early life living with my grandmother in Colliers Row at Tirphil during the Second World War. My brother Lawrence and I were sent back to Wales by our parents to avoid the London bombing, they having moved the family to London when I was three years old.

Lawrence went to Bargoed Technical and I went to Tirphil Boys' School, known as the 'Tin Hut'. We both initially had a hard time because of our Cockney accents but the Welsh lilt soon returned to our voices. School dinners in most schools could be a disaster but not in Tirphil. We all went to the girls' school and were fed really great food from a kitchen, supervised by Mabel Coleman who was apparently a Tirphil local celebrity, having once married into the Tate & Lyle sugar family.

'School Street, The Square, The Working Men's Institute, Birch Grove. The Home Guard practising up the mountains.'

Gran Hannan ran an open house where it was quite normal for us to come home from the sports field late in the evening to find ten or twelve people sitting around waiting for the local bus. Gran's son Tom was living with his mother and worked as a tailor, carrying out repairs to all forms of clothing for the local people. The house was treated as a haven for all sorts of local people and there could not have been too many people in Tirphil who didn't know Kate and Tom.

In my later years the memories come flooding back. School Street, The Square, The Working Men's Institute, Birch Grove. The Home Guard practising up the mountains. Wallbioff the Butchers and the Railway Station which always had an advert for Cadburys Chocolate together with an advert for Camp Coffee, why should I remember that? The local milk was delivered by 'Tommy the Milk' whose father had a farm near Pontlotin. When he went down the hill he had to change the harness so that the cart went before the horse. He served his milk directly from a churn in a mug-like utensil called a gill.

To say these days were the happiest of our lives would be untrue. Although Tirphil kept us away from the London Blitz, we were always aware that we were away from our parents and older siblings. However, even today after some sixty-five years I still hold fond memories of Tirphil, and how it taught me the history of my homeland and its love of music and rugby, the kindness of valley people and the joy I have today watching Welsh rugby and wearing the 'red shirt' of Wales.

*Thomas Shorey* 93031

## Terrified by white masses!

I was taken to the upper Rhondda Valley (Tynewydd) by my mother in 1940 during the war, I was some 9 years old. My mum worked all through the war in the weapons factory at Bridgend so I grew up in a mining area and I have never forgotten it. Being from the south coast (Bournemouth), the blackness of everything really shocked me. Well, the other thing that has remained in my memory is that when arriving at Blaenrhondda station all I could see was huge 'white masses in the sky', it took a long time to get me off the train. My first sight of mountains - I was terrified!

*Ray Paget* 217711

## The bomb at Ynysddu

I was born in number 1 Bridge Street at Ynysddu in 1935. My memory relates to 1941, when I sat on the bedroom window sill and watched the buses of evacuees being taken from the Station Hotel road after arriving at the railway station. I also remember a huge bomb being displayed in the Ambulance Hall but I can't remember the year.

*Grahame Tanner* 207054

## The sooty rice pudding at Grangetown, Cardiff

*'Dad just took the pudding off her, scraped the soot off and dished it up.'*

I lived in Grangetown as a child. We never had much money, my dad worked hard in Grange Clinic and down the Marl as caretaker, and my mum did little jobs to try to help, but we always had holes in our shoes unless Dad could scrounge a bit of leather to repair them. I always remember Mum telling me about the night the Plymouth Arms pub was blown up by a dropped bomb during the war. Dad had just got in from fire-watch when it happened. Mum had a rice pudding in the hob oven by the fire and the door of the oven flew open and all the soot went all over the pudding from the blast of the bomb - we only lived a few doors from the pub. Mum wanted to get rid of it but Dad just took it off her, scraped the soot off and dished it up. I was only a baby then but it still makes me smile to remember.

*Ralph Spackman* 112441

## I was evacuated to Gilfach Goch

I was aged 7 when we first arrived. We were separated into different families. I stayed with my mum, at Mrs John's, who we all called 'Mum John'. The family was very nice; the son Glyn worked in the pits. A very vivid memory was seeing Glyn arrive back from work with a black face, arms and hands, and washing in a tin bath in the living room, while everyone went about their business.

I went to the local school and came top in Welsh! The headmaster was furious, and scolded the locals. I picked up a strong Welsh accent but soon lost it again on returning to London.

I really enjoyed my stay in Gilfach Goch, and the people there made it very happy.

*Sally 105561*

*'Seeing Glyn arrive back from work with a black face, arms and hands, and washing in a tin bath in the living room, while everyone went about their business.'*

## My memories of Gilfach Goch in the war

During the war years my mother frequently cooked the meals for the soldiers serving on a searchlight unit up near the farms on Sunday, and they kindly cut off a piece of meat joint for her to provide the meat for our Sunday dinner. Given the extent of the rationing, this was very much appreciated.

I also remember when I went up to the searchlight unit one night during the early 1940s and was allowed to control the searchlight to try and spot a German bomber flying over the village. However, as a young boy of only 10 or 11 years old I didn't have the strength to adequately control the searchlight, which was flashing across the sky and not focusing on the German aircraft flying overhead. One of the soldiers therefore took control of the searchlight and focused on it, and a number of other searchlights then focused on it and highlighted the German bomber.

I have some very pleasant memories of my childhood spent in Gilfach Goch, and of the war years.

*Dilwyn Hardwidge 261941*

## I was evacuated to Llanbradach

My grandparents, Ben and Polly Thomas, ran the pub opposite the Miners' Welfare at Llanbradach. I was evacuated there and I remember how on Saturday nights the US Servicemen would come along with their band and play in the pub. There was the bottom bar, the top bar (posh bar) and the Snug out the back. My grandparents had a white-haired terrier called 'Tim'. Tim would come into the bar, the bottom bar where the widows of miners were allowed in on Saturday nights. Tim would go into the middle of the bar carrying an enamel bucket with a wooden handle. He would swing the bucket around and then let it go, run and jump over the bar and race out the back. My grandparents did not like cats but had to have one for the mice in the cellars. They called the cat 'Hitler'. It was fun to see in the cellars a mouse come round the corner with Hitler chasing and Tim chasing Hitler – just like 'Tom and Jerry'.

I remember that whilst I lived there I was given a flute which I blew, but the Police Station next door took exception as it just sounded like a police whistle!

One final story, the Snug bar of the pub stayed open to 1am, and many a Saturday night with no transport about they often found a cow, put the drinker on the cow and led him home. I met a gentleman in Sevenoaks who remembered being one of the guests on board the cow, he was taken to Caerphilly, then let the cow loose which walked back to Llanbradach!

*John Rooke 51751*

*'They often found a cow, put the drinker on the cow and led him home.'*

LLANBRADACH, Main Street c1955 L283006

## The old primary school at Gilwern

I attended the old primary school via School Lane through the 1930s and early 1940s. The school by the old canal was a very happy school, and through the last war we had a big school garden where we grew food and shared it in the village. We also had to help on the local farm (Jim Llewellyn's, at Ty Gwyn) at potato picking time, we had good food and got paid – we enjoyed that. I left school in 1945 but enjoyed my years there.

*George Evans 87201*

## Our schooldays memories of Upper Cwmbran

I was born in Church Road, Pontnewydd, in 1935, we moved to Ty-Pwca Road in 1947. I attended Upper Cwmbran School and well remember the fun we had there. Gardening lessons with the Head, Mr Jones – 'Clear the weeds, boys, and sow the seeds carefully in straight rows', he would say. The friends made then are still friends though some have, sadly, departed this life. My memories include Siloam Chapel, the golf links, Slippery Path, the Mountain Air pub and games with friends in the wood behind Ty-Pwca Road. I also remember the fun we had as the steel houses were erected, and the arctic winter of 1947/48 and having to walk along a single track in the snow of four feet deep up Trappers Hill and into Pontnewydd village centre to buy bread. Many, many, many memories. Those were good, 'honest' days.

*Lance Ford 28391*

*'Clear the weeds, boys, and sow the seeds carefully in straight rows.'*

I lived at the back of Ty-Pwca Road steel houses in Wentwood Close from 1952 to 1971 and went to Upper Cwmbran School from 1952-59 and the class was in the middle room of the building on the upper floor. There was an old coke stove at the front end of the classroom, to keep us warm in winter, which was topped up by removing the round lid on top. Just down from the school was a corner shop, Lewis's, where we used to buy sweets on our way to the school, and up the lane was a small park and the golf links which are still there. If we were early enough to the school playground and it was dry there was a game of football going on which everyone who wanted to could join in. The end of the school day, 4pm, was signalled by one of the children ringing a handbell.

*Dave Standing 150611*

WHITEBROOK, Tump Farm and the Valley from the Main Road c1960 W636006

## Memories from the Morris family of The Gristmill, Whitebrook

A story I would like to share is that as a child my dad used to catch the train from Whitebrook to Monmouth for school. He and his brothers often returned home pleading 'Sorry Mum, can't go to school, we missed the train'. After a few weeks, unknown to them, my grandmother changed all the clocks in the house back by an hour – so when they next said they'd missed the train, she grabbed them by the ears and frog-marched them to the waiting train! Another story is that they played Cowboys and Indians in the woods and used to fire catapults and bows and arrows across the (White) brook at each other. Although always forbidden, this was their greatest game. It stopped when Jack got an arrow fired directly into his eye. The kids didn't need to be told then, they believed the doctor that Jack would be blind and were petrified, yet somehow his sight remained intact. But it was a wonderful story repeated with much laughter and guffawing at all family occasions for the next 50 years.

*Ruth Wolveridge* 204462

## Learning right from wrong at Pontnewydd Church School in the 1940s

As I remember, the discipline there was tough, but at least you knew right from wrong and if you did something wrong you could expect punishment – nearly always the cane. We all had to attend the church for assembly once a week and were marched there from our lines in the playground. At other times, except in bad weather when the interior glass panelled walls were pushed back to form a huge hall, we stood in our class lines in the yard and sang our hymn – the words for which were on a colourful roll of material suspended from the high windows. Lessons were generally silent. The teacher would explain what was to be done in that lesson, give three examples on the blackboard, then tell us what page to turn to in our 1920s' text books and we were told to get on with it. Each day two boys were despatched to deliver the milk, in third of a pint bottles, to each classroom.

*Lance Ford 172111*

## My schooldays at Caerleon Endowed School

Our family moved to Brook Cottage, Llandegveth, in about 1945 when Dad went to work for Mr Joe Shepherd at Ty Capten Farm, and my three brothers, Arthur, David, Noel and I would catch the canvas-covered charabanc (bus) to Caerleon school. The Headmaster was Mr Lovatt and the bus belonged to Mark Howells Ltd of Caerleon. Noel and I, being the youngest, were in the infants and the worrying part was having to go to bed in the afternoon on canvas camp beds in the classroom. No-one told me that we would be packed off home at the required time, and as a result I would lie terrified that the bus with Arthur and David on it would go and leave Noel and I behind!

*Robert Bassett 282151*

## Plasticine animals and warm milk – memories of school in the 1940s at Ynysboeth, in the Cynon Valley

I remember my first day at Ynysboeth Infants School, and unceremoniously being dragged there by my mother for the first time, because I didn't want to go to school. However, as I was happily greeted by the teacher on entering the classroom for the first time, I also saw this wonderful huge rocking horse directly in front of me with one seat fixed at the front, and the other at the back of the horse. What I loved most, at that very tender age, was making animals out of Plasticine, especially elephants. Even to this day I can still smell that Plasticine. But there was a smell I hated, which was when we had to drink from the small bottles of milk after they were heated on the radiators in the classroom during the winter months.

*Royden Jones 204309*

## 'Up the Baths' at Brynmawr

I remember being 'taught to swim' here in the 1960s, by the teachers at the board school. We were stood at the poolside, only up to the black line, then were summarily told to 'Jump!'. If that failed, we were helped in by the boot of 'Danny' Davis or 'Joe' Robbins, then expected to 'swim' back to shallow water. I had great times in those summers.

*Michael Evans* 117331

*'If that failed, we were helped in by the boot of 'Danny' Davis or 'Joe' Robbins.'*

BRYNMAWR, The Swimming Pool c1955 B730052

## Good days at New Tredegar

I went to New Tredegar Technical School from 1962 to 1967. It was a good time. I lived in Phillipstown and it was a 10 minute walk to school – fantastic. I remember the bad winter of 1963 and my satchel was ruined by the sleighing down the hill to school (the excuse I made to my parents was worthy of an Oscar). The Tech had good teachers (Mining Institute effect) and it was a very close community. It was overseen by the head (Mr Stanley Jones), he was strict but fair. One day a prank was done on the staff and SJ. Their rooms were next to each other, and opposite was a banister leading up the stairs (an anchor point). Some sharp person, using the knowledge from physics lessons regarding levers, tied a rope around each door knob and around the banister, then banged hard on each door. We watched the comedy unravel – it was like a Norman Wisdom film, as each of them pulled and pushed. Remember, it was after all a Technical School (applied science)!

*'We watched the comedy unravel – it was like a Norman Wisdom film, as each of them pulled and pushed.'*

*Howard Watkins* 378541

## A well-remembered teacher at Tondu

I went to the old Tondu Junior School, now sadly knocked down, and also went to the old infants school that was next to the junior school. We used to stand by the railings next to the brick works and when they opened up the kilns we used to get the heat on our faces through the railings. School was not for me though, and it was only due to one teacher that I left school able to read and write, and that was Mr Chilcott, a teacher that spent his time with us to help us.

*David Berry* 197971

# My schoolday memoirs from the Trowbridge/ St Mellons area of Cardiff, 1964-1966

I was just over 2 years old when my family and I moved to 39 Hendre Road, Trowbridge Estate, St Mellons, Cardiff. I recall all we had to sit on was a few tea chests. Hendre Road itself was a dirt track, and there were no pavements, our garden was a furrowed field, it looked like a building site. Our house had cast concrete walls, they don't make houses like that these days. I used to watch them build the flat roofed pre-fab houses; each wall panel slid into place using a crane.

I recall how terrified I was on that day I started at Trowbridge Infant School in Tresigin Road, when my mum left me alone. I remember the smell of school dinners, and there was a tyre and log in the playground I used to play on. One day the teacher stopped me from going to lunch because I was behind on maths; my mum attended the school and had a go at the teacher. At the Christmas party, we had to take our own spoon, knife and folk with our names on, and a food contribution for the party; I took a tin of fruit cocktail. I recall Caroline Chaplin; we would be given a rich tea biscuit and a quart of milk daily, Caroline would always pencil on her biscuit then eat it.

Later I attended Greenway Junior School in Towen Road, Rumney. I would help Mr Lewis the caretaker just to get extra milk. In school dinners I'd have seconds, and pudding. My mum used to give me the bus fare of 2d there and 2d back, but I'd walk to and home from school and spend the money on sweets.

*Wayne Carter 231031*

*'My mum used to give me the bus fare of 2d there and 2d back, but I'd walk to and home from school and spend the money on sweets.'*

## The kids at Ffaldau Primary at Pontycymer were great...

I loved the Square at Pontycymer, and watching the coal miners sit and talk and smoke. I miss the valley, I have been in the USA since 1982. I loved my time teaching at Ffaldau Primary from 1971 to 1982. The kids and parents were great.

*Dai Harris* 284761

## ...I was one of them!

Hello Mr Harris, I remember you at Ffaldau; you were always giving me a row for one thing or another. I guess you could say I was not your best pupil, I did not like to listen and hated being told what to do (nothing much has changed!). I remember my youngest brother had to wait for me outside the classroom at home time (for me to take him home), he would always make faces at us and make us laugh, so in the end you would let him in to wait. You also had myself and Tracy Hart drink two bottles of milk a day to help us grow, because we were so short. I don't know about Tracy but I'm still short! I hope you don't mind the memories because to me, they were the best. I loved my years at Ffaldau Juniors.

*Carolyne Jones* 363711

*'Watching the coal miners sit and talk and smoke.'*

PONTYCYMER, The Square c1955 P227007

## We went home as smoked as kippers...

I was born and brought up in the tiny village of Manmoel on top of the mountain between Cwm and Hollybush south of Ebbw Vale. My dad, George, was a farmer in the area until his death in 1978. It was a wonderful childhood - until I was 13, I thought everyone was an aunt or uncle. I went to Sunday school in the Chapel and Christmas parties in the old school (closed in 1952). My friends were Clive Burgess and Wynford Penny and we shot more Germans than the 8th Army and more Indians than John Wayne in the fields and woods around the village. The sheep pound near Tonyfald Farm was either the Alamo or Beau Geste's desert fort. We dug cabins in the earth covered with corrugated iron sheets and turf, filled the insides full of dried ferns and then - lit a camp fire inside! We went home as smoked as kippers. *Glyn Davies 82401*

RISCA, The Canal from Darren Bridge c1955 R328010

## Playing on the canal at Risca

I spent many happy days here with my brother and sister. Playing in home-made boats made from corrugated tin, catching tadpoles and skating on very thin ice in the winter. I lived in Woodview Road and my grandparents lived in Mount Pleasant.

*Virginia Kidd 91681*

## This photograph takes me back!

In this picture, the post in the middle of the path is an old cannon barrel. When I went for walks along this canal as a kid, I can remember running on a short distance ahead of my parents with my brother and sister to the cannon barrel to see how much dirt and gravel we could gather up and shove down the end of it before my parents caught up with us.

The house in the distance is Fernlea, and the picture is taken from the canal path outside the 'Prince of Wales' public house.

*Martin Blandford 91901*

*'We'd see how much dirt and gravel we could gather up and shove down the end of it.'*

PONTYMISTER, Twm Barlwm from the Canal c1955 P309007

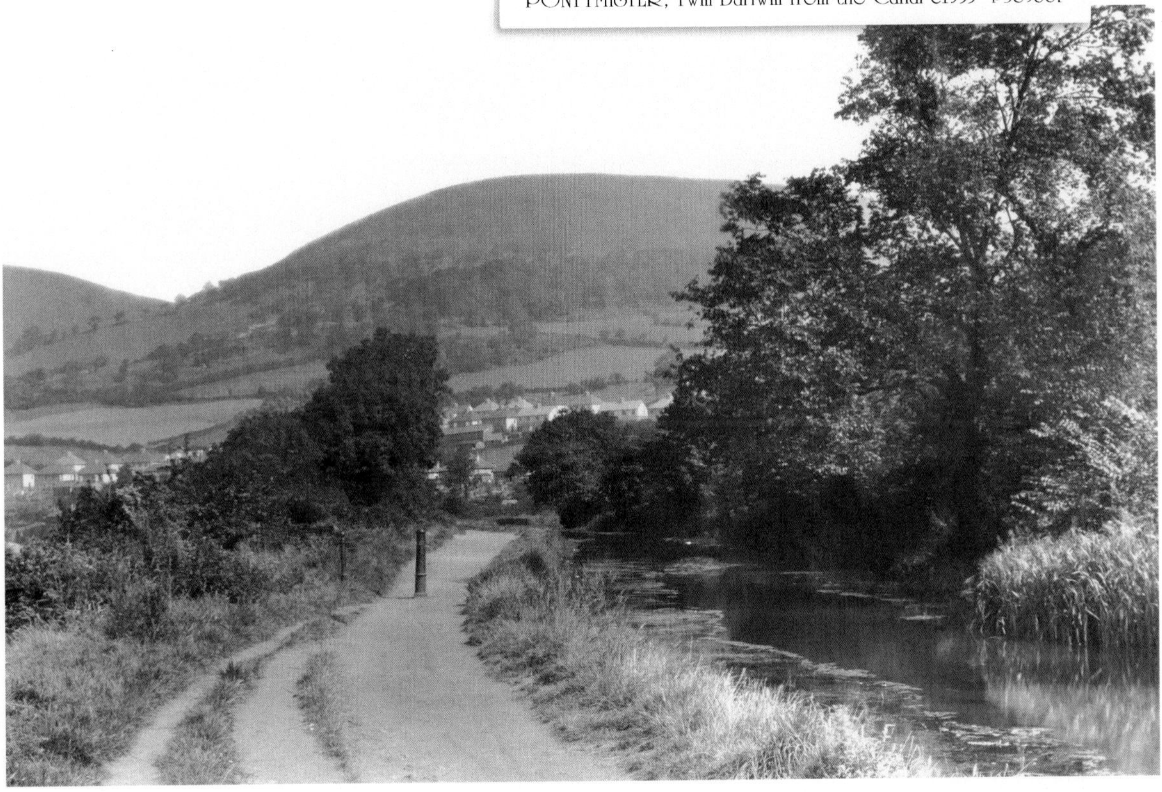

## Innocent days at New Tredegar

I remember innocent days playing football on Grove Park until you could hardly see the ball. I lived in Greenfield Street and recall tying a piece of string from behind the garden wall to the fence on the back lane and sitting in wait for someone to come along to trip up, and in the winter we would slide down the three corners dumps on cardboard. We never had a lot but it was always an adventure, except for the fact that I lived in 153 Greenfield Street and we always seemed to get flooded. Mind you, one year we were planning to go to Barry Island for a treat, when we got up in the morning there was at least two foot of water downstairs. Mam said 'Well, come on, we are still going, we can worry about it when we get home', and off we went and caught the train from White Rose train station; when we got home after having a great time, the water had gone down. I remember the milk women coming around and filling up our jugs and the photographer's van where you would sit in the back and have your photo taken, and watching the greyhounds running around the Grove Park. My job was to catch the hare before the dogs got to it. We had no computers or fancy games, just our imagination – how things change.

*Robert Kendrick* 123811

*'Well, come on, we are still going, we can worry about it when we get home.'*

## Heaven at the Lido at Allt-yr-yn, Newport

I lived in Blean-y-pant Crescent and we would walk along the canal towpath to reach the Lido. The Lido was heaven to us kids. The mums would pack sandwiches and sometimes buy us a packet of crisps. There were 2 kinds, plain with a blue paper twist of salt or the exotic Oxo flavour – they were my favourite! We would have to sit and wait at least half an hour after eating before swimming for fear of drowning. The place teemed with children. We would play in the clear sparkling water until our mums dragged us home. Glory days!

*Sharon Challingsworth* 379251

## Riding the buckets and other daft things at Aberbargoed in the 1960s

I remember when we would ride the buckets from Bargoed Pit to Brittania across the river, playing on our big rope swing by Angel Lane and teasing the Pit Bobby. How we survived I'll never know. I think we learned more about elf'n safety the natural way than all the over-paid 'experts' could in a lifetime of courses that they have attended, and I'm still kicking in my middle age...

*Peter Szmytki 98521*

> *'I think we learned more about elf'n safety the natural way than all the over-paid 'experts' could in a lifetime.'*

## Sliding at Aberbargoed

I remember sliding down the quarry on Markham Road at Aberbargoed. When I got to the bottom a man gave me a clout for being so daft. I bet he would not get away with that nowadays!

*Lyndon Gingell 22391*

## Shortchanging the church collection at Penygraig in the Rhondda Valley...

We used to go to church at St Barnabas at Penygraig and on the way home we were allowed to buy sweets at the little sweet shop by the church, I think it was called Marian's. One week my mum got mad because instead of putting in 6 pence for collection I put it in and than took out 3 pence change for extra sweets! Yumm, Blackjacks, Palmer Violets, Sherbert Dabs, Bazooka Joe bubble gum and so on...

*Jan Thomas 26761*

## Playing on the 'swinging bridge' and stepping stones at Merthyr Mawr and Ogmore, near Bridgend

What a 'swinging bridge' it was at Merthyr Mawr back in the 1950s! I don't know when it was changed to a 'solid' bridge, but how it ever survived the rough handling that we boys from the 'Cottage Homes' on the Merthyr Mawr Road at Bridgend gave it every year...Well! Amazing! We would walk down the lanes from the 'Homes', past 'Island Farm' POW Camp, then on past 'Bluebell Woods' and 'Primrose Woods' (if there were girls with us, we'd detour into the woods, quite innocent really!), then on again past all those beautiful conker trees (which we scrumped every year), the tennis club, and then to the village. Does anyone remember the very big 'punching tree'? We used to get all the younger boys to punch it, to show them that it was indeed possible to hit it hard without hurting your hands! It was in front of that big house on the main road, or was it the church? The tree still had a patch of missing bark the last time I saw it! OK, now onto the bridge! We would pack as many boys as possible onto it, and swing in unison, side to side, until the restraining hawser twanged to a point that frightened us to death, then stopped. Somewhere in the back of my mind, I believe that there was a time that a restraining hawser was not used! But that might be wishful thinking! We didn't finish there! Oh no, we still had the stepping stones over the river at Ogmore to go! Quite a few duckings were had there, I can tell you! And I have known us to take any 'New Boys' across the stones, at a point where the tide was fast approaching 'Top Tide', then run back over to the Merthyr Mawr side and throw stones at them, until they could only go back to Bridgend, the long way round. We still had two options left! Back to Merthyr Mawr, and on to the sandhills, or else join the other boys on the 'wrong side' and go on to Ogmore by Sea, and see what mischief we could get up to there! I tell people who express pity about us 'Cottage Homes Kids' that we had a whale of a time! If I had my life over again, I wouldn't change a day.

*Terry Evans 130691*

## I saw the old 'swinging bridge's' destruction...

I saw the old swinging bridge's destruction at Merthyr Mawr. It was during the big flood of the 1960s when trees were washed down and ended up tangled to what was left of it. The suspension bridge was built a few years after that – sadly, nowhere near the fun of the proper 'swinging bridge'.

*Robert Edmunds 181961*

OGMORE, Old Cottage and Stepping Stones 1937 87993

*'We used to get all the younger boys to punch it, to show them that it was indeed possible to hit it hard without hurting your hands!'*

## Going to the pictures at Ystrad Mynach, in the Rhymney Valley

Who can remember going to the Saturday morning pictures at Ystrad Mynach? We would see films like 'Annie Get your Gun' and 'An American in Paris', followed by the wonderful 'Captain Marvel' etc. My friends and I would often act out bits from the movies, singing and dancing on the Pierhead, which gave us a wonderfully natural stage on which to perform. What a strange piece of architecture it is. I'm glad that it's still there. If you see someone taking photos of that and other pieces of Ystrad it might be me!

*Ann (née Webb)* 179171

YSTRAD MYNACH, The Village 1938 88705

MOUNTAIN ASH, Town Hall and Bridge 1950 M175020

## Watching the steam trains at Mountain Ash

I lived on Llanwonno Road in Mountain Ash in the 1960s. Every Sunday I would cross this bridge with my elder brother Kenneth, on our way to the Baptist Chapel. This was the time of steam trains. We could hear the trains coming a long time before they reached the bridge. When we heard the train we used to run to where the train ran underneath, lean over the edge of the bridge, and get lost in the white smoke and steam from the train as it trundled along below, a time when it seemed like a different world full of amazing things with these magical machine monsters.

*Peter Weeks 204094*

*'We used to run to where the train ran underneath, lean over the edge of the bridge, and get lost in the white smoke and steam from the train.'*

## My wonderful childhood at Caerau

I was born at 87 Victoria Street at Caerau in 1945. My father was a miner and worked all his life in Caerau colliery. At the age of 3 we moved from Victoria Street to Bryn Terrace with a lovely view of Caerau and the Llynfi valley. Looking back, my childhood was spent most of the time outdoors in all weathers and the long hot summer days of the 1950s seemed to go on for ever, every day was an adventure. We all wore short trousers in the 1950s and spent all our time running over the mountains, making dens and flying home-made kites. I can remember as a small boy walking through Victoria Street and looking at all the milk bottles placed outside the doors and some of them had money left in them, in those days you would buy an orange disc from the Co-operative store, if you left out two discs then the milkman would leave you two pints of milk, if you had no orange checks left then you would leave out the money for the milk. My friends and I never had two pennies to rub together yet we would never ever dream of taking that money. It was a time of respect and honesty. I have such happy wonderful memories that I cherish. I can remember walking the mountains with the skylark singing in flight, and the whinberry picking all day on the mountain, when you were filling your box of whinberries it was pick one and eat two, our lips would be purple by the time we filled the box and then there was that delicious whinberry pie that your mother made.

I still live in Caerau. I have seen many changes in my life, and I often think back about how we made our own fun like 'kick the tin', when one boy would kick the tin and give us enough time to hide. We had a lot of respect for the elders of the village. It was a time when you left your front door key hanging on a piece of string in the letter box. Everybody knew each other, the neighbours had a sense of belonging and there seemed to be a genuine air of humility among the people. Although many found it hard to make ends meet, there was a clear spirit of generosity with the people of Caerau.

*Colin Evans 122181*

## Making lead soldiers and flattening halfpennies – playing at Caerau in the 1950s

I remember playing on a pit heap behind Evans Terrace at Caerau and watching older lads make lead soldiers from small moulds they carried around. They melted the lead on fires made from coal picked from the heap. I also used to trek up the mountain with other kids to camp and also catch newts in the pit ponds. The steam trains ran up the valley at the time and we used to put halfpennies on the line to flatten them. *Glynne Lewis 232011*

CAERAU, General View c1955 C387015

## Hanging off the back of the bus at Penrhiwceiber in the Cynon Valley

I was born in Perthcelyn, near Penrhiwceiber, in 1955 at 8 Hawthorn Terrace (corner of Brynheulog). One thing we used to do as kids was hang off the back of the bus as it stopped on the corner and jump off at Moore's at the top of the hill – if it didn't stop you were hanging on for dear life until you got to the Miskin. If we were really scared we used to open the back door and the alarm would sound, causing the driver to stop, and we would jump off and run away. No regard to H&S in those days!

*David Goodman* 290941

## Diving off the Donkey Rock at Rotherslade Bay

We moved to Thistleboon, Mumbles from the East End of London in 1968 when I was 7 years old and I fell in love with the sea. A fond memory of those far off summers is of my friends and I jumping from the Donkey Rock at Rotherslade at high tide. You had to time your launch just right to catch the crest of a wave as it rolled up the beach... too soon and the water would be too shallow, many a scraped knee or ankle was had from these escapades. It was particularly good if there had been a storm the day before and the surf was choked with seaweed. This would act as a cushion upon landing! Mind you... it was a bit of a struggle getting out to the beach. Today's Health & Safety police would have a fit if they saw what we got up to when we were young. I remember tying old washing lines together and abseiling down the cliffs at Lambs Well and Doctors Mine, and one Bonfire Night we collected as many fireworks as we could, packed all the gunpowder from them into an old Coke can, piled pebbles from the beach around and blew it up under the old Rotherslade concrete promenade... the resulting boom left me deaf for 3 days afterwards and I've still got the scar on my head where the blast knocked me over. Ahh... happy days and a charmed childhood.

*Jeff Horton* 132631

## Clearing the footpaths at Abercarn

My grandfather was a miner in the South Celynen. He started off at the age of 13 and was made redundant when the mines closed. But what's more interesting about him was that he had two hobbies. One was a love for repairing old clocks and watches and the second, and the more interesting to me, was his love of walking. My mother would take me and my brother down to visit every other Saturday where we would go walking whatever the weather and today we still walk some of the paths he used to take us along. But it wasn't until he passed away that we discovered a local councillor would pay him half a crown to keep the paths open. I remember him removing the overgrowth as we walked and even moving fences when the farmer had blocked a path!

*Teresa Hughes* 380291

## Life at Gellideg Isaf Farm, Maesycwmmer

I was born in 1958, on the farm named Gellideg Isaf of which now sadly only the farmhouse exists. The farm in 1958 had some twenty one acres, and as I got to the age of eight I started to help my parents with the haymaking during the hot summer months. I have great memories of people from all over the village, who would come and join in, to be rewarded with cider and Welsh cakes after they had done the hard work. These were great days, which will always remain in my memory. Thanks to my parents (Malcolm and Milly).

*Roy Williams* 48301

*'I have great memories of people from all over the village, who would come and join in, to be rewarded with cider and Welsh cakes after they had done the hard work.'*

## Send Grandad some fresh air!

My mother's parents lived in Lloyd Street at Caerau for many years. Grandad, known by me, I am told, as 'Dampa', was a coal miner at the pit up the hill from Lloyd Street and I remember him showing me the pit ponies (recently retired as they had put a railway up to the pithead). Dampa passed away in the late 1950s from the then common 'miners' disease', lack of breath. I remember he had a hand bellows to help his breathing and always joked with us about sending him a tin of clean air from Portsmouth where we lived.

*Harry Alford* 51561

## My memories of Pontlottyn cinema

I have great memories of Pontlottyn cinema in the 1960s, my mam didn't have much money but she always managed to give us sixpence every Friday to go to the cinema. I remember Mrs Jones coming around with her torch, if we so much as sneezed the light would be straight on us with a warning that if we didn't keep quiet we'd be out. And there was a few times we were put out! She later worked in Pontlottyn toilets and when we went in she was completely different, she'd call us into the little room she occupied with a little gas fire and talk with us and was very friendly, what a difference from the stern woman who petrified us at the cinema. Ah, those were the days. We didn't have a lot but they were great times.

*June Williams* 206417

## The generous miners of Llanbradach

My grandparents lived in Rees Terrace at Llanbradach. My grandfather Hugh Price Watkins was the St John Ambulance driver for the mines and I spent every summer and most weekends in Llanbradach and went to school there for three months while my mother was in hospital in Merthyr. Whenever I walked past the pub on the corner opposite the Miners' Welfare with my grandfather, the miners who were gathered outside always used to put a penny or halfpenny in my hand, which even at the age of 10 I did not want to take as I knew they did not have a lot of money. They insisted I took it as they said: 'Your grandfather looks after us when we get injured.'

*'Don't go down the pit, Bach.'*

Whenever there was an accident in the mines, the phone would ring in Grandad's house and I would be told the location of the accident and would run as fast as my legs would carry me to the garage right next to the bridge by the station. After picking up another man, I would accompany them in the ambulance to the accident site and would often ride in the back of the ambulance with the injured pitman, not something that Health & Safety would allow now. Without exception they would say to me: 'Don't go down the pit, Bach.' I didn't.

*Lionel Drew 222031/221771*

# I used to travel on this bus...

I was born in Brynmawr. I was not brought up there but all my relatives lived there and still do to this day. This photo of the Market Square and the old bus brings back memories of trips from Dany-yr-Park to Brynmawr – in that same bus, driven by a chap called Harry (I think). I was only 10 years old at the time and it was the most exciting trip through Gilwern, past Clydach and up Black Rock incline. Everything was a wonderment to a 10-year-old. Sometimes the bus ran parallel with the steam train – I never got to travel on the train, but oh, how I wanted to. (Unfortunately Dr Beeching closed it all down.) But I waved like mad at the train and wished that I was on it. Arrival at the Square was always an anticlimax but also a sense of awe. Here was the big city in all its grandeur (or so it seemed to an impressionable 10-year-old). I'd wander about for an hour, go to the market and get a bag of sweets for 3 pence, go see my grandfather Robin who didn't really want to see me and made it patently clear that I was not welcome (grumpy old beggar). From there to my auntie's home where I was welcome, eat some home-made cake and ginger beer, spend some time down the Welfare park and on to the cinema which had the usual Western on. After the movie, I grabbed a bag of chips and wandered off home to my auntie's. Wonderful memories.

*David Palfrey 20481*

BRYNMAWR, The Market Square c1955 B730071

## Happy days at the Dingle at Aberbeeg in the Ebbw Valley

Our family never went out of Aberbeeg for holidays except for the odd trip to Barry with the chapel. So every summer we went to the Dingle a lot with my cousins and aunties. We would pack food and swimming costumes but we never took drinks as we would fill our empty Corona bottles with the sweet, cold spring water that poured out of the mountain. We walked through the Square, under the bridge, past Mrs Cook's and Kibby's on towards the Dingle. We picked wimberries and bluebells, swam in the reza and splashed about in the stream all day whilst our mam and aunties looked on. At the end of the day, when the sun had gone from this lovely valley and was only shining on the tops of the beautiful fir trees, our mam made us tip our jars of tadpoles back in the stream and the older boys had caught trout. I would take my soggy dress that had been tucked in my soggy knickers and reluctantly put on my soggy daps (plimsoles) to wend our way home. I always ate my wimberries walking home, ending up with a purple tongue and lips and my mam saying 'Oh Jilly, you look a sight for sore eyes', but I had never been happier.

*Jill Galloway* 394831

*'We walked through the Square, under the bridge, past Mrs Cook's and Kibby's on towards the Dingle.'*

## When the whistles blew at Blaenllechau on New Year's Eve...

One of my earliest memories is of New Year's Eve in the mid-1950s when I was five or six, and my mother and father got me up from bed to hear the whistles of the trains in the siding blow at midnight. We stood on the door hand in hand, the night was cold and the sky clear. The stars twinkled and shone like mercury on velvet. When the whistles fell silent we went inside and my father had a beer, my mother probably a sherry and I had a glass of home-made ginger beer.

*John Howe* 240591

## Trips on the steam trains

My best memories from my childhood at Caerau are of our train rides to Cymmer, when steam trains were the normal means of transport, with our pocket money on a Saturday. We would try to have a seated area to ourselves, open the windows and try to fill the carriage with smoke as we passed through the tunnel. Sometimes we took the train to Maesteg. In the holiday season, the family day out would be to Porthcawl, changing trains at Tondu, or at times taking the train to Barry, changing at Cardiff. Every journey was a blessing to me (and still is in a steam train today).

*David Walters 173461*

## Sunday outings to my grandparents in the 1940s

I remember travelling over to Nantymoel in an Austin 7 from the Western Valley. It was very cramped with my mother and father, younger brother and a friend of the family. This was a regular family outing to see my grandparents, William H Thomas and Mary Jane Thomas, who lived in 57 Station Road. It was the very last house in the road. It was always a special Sunday treat for the family.

It was always a thrill to reach the top of the Bwlch and see the valley below. We were always treated to a fine meal and afterwards I would play outside with the neighbour's children. I remember that one of the other children was Lynn Davies who later became famous as an athlete. (Born in Nantymoel in 1942, Lynn Davies won an Olympic gold medal in the long jump in 1964, earning himself the nickname 'Lynn the Leap'.)

We would often be joined by relatives who lived locally. The adults would gather in the parlour and my grandmother would play the piano. I remember that the room would get very smoky.

*David Thomas 37421*

## The joys of knitted bathing trunks in the 1950s...

I can remember wearing knitted bathing trunks. We all went to Porthcawl with the church trip from our home in Caerau, once you went into the sea the knitted bathing trunks became wet and heavy and hanged down, and it was all we could do to walk holding them up.

*Colin Evans 122181*

## Happy days at Abercwmboi, near Mountain Ash, in the early 1950s

We used to live in 3 Cromer Street, with my dad's Uncle Bert. If memory serves, Bert used to work at the Phurnacite Plant, but my overriding memory is of him selling Corona pop from the house. He must have had a franchise of some sort, as there were always crates of the stuff under the stairs and a Corona lorry used to bring the new stock. Next door down (number 2) was a Mrs Roberts and up the street I remember Mrs Sweet and, a lovely old chap, Mr Jones (I can't remember who lived where, but, one was number 5 and the other number 8). Mr Jones was an old collier and used to make me boats out of his 'blocks' (the timber that colliers brought home for firewood). We'd walk down Cromer Street, across the main road and then down between the Co-op and the (then) abattoir to sail these 'block' boats on the pond in this photograph - leaving a wake through the coal dust on the surface. They were hard times in the early fifties and my mum used to take my old pram down to the tip by the pond to pick coal from amongst the slag, it was common practice and there would often be a group of women there scavenging for what little coal there was on the tip.

Bert used to be a keen gardener and we were never short of fresh fruit and veg from his garden. Mr Jones kept chickens, I remember, and someone else further up the street kept pigs.

We moved to Cwmbach in 1952 but I've always had happy memories of Abercwmboi - despite the poverty and shortages, they were Happy Days. And, YES, people did leave their front doors open, it was a warm and close community. How things change. *Allan Jones 79871*

ABERCWMBOI, The Phurnacite Plant c1955 A190001

## The smoke from the Phurnacite Plant was the first thing I saw every morning...

The first time I saw this photo (opposite) on the Frith website it brought back very old memories, because when I got up from bed in the mornings and opened my curtains the first thing I saw was the smoke from the Phurnacite Plant, as we lived in Park View Terrace which was not more than a few hundred yards from the site. The pond in the picture was where we used to swim in the summer and also we did some fishing in the same pond. My memory of the men that worked at the plant was they had to put on this yellow cream on their faces so that the tar would not burn their faces. There were some men who worked on coke ovens who had to wear wooden clogs because the heat from the coke ovens was so hot that if they had only everyday working boots they would have burnt away because of the heat. Thankfully the Phurnacite Plant is no longer throwing out its smoke and smells any more.

*David Williams 35051*

## My happy memories of Abercwmboi

*'It was safe for children to go out in the dark then.'*

I was born in Abercwmboi in 1954 but my parents moved south in 1956. We returned there several times every year, staying with my grandparents, Eddie and Sue Milton, at 39 Bronnallt Terrace every Christmas and again for several weeks during the summer. The last week was always spent in a caravan at Porthcawl, the best holidays I have ever had. I have so many wonderful memories of Abercwmboi, especially of going from house to house on New Year's Eve just after the clock struck midnight, calling 'Happy New Year' through all the letterboxes. Everyone would come out and hand us a few pennies for the New Year, it was safe for children to go out in the dark then. I remember looking across the lake at the lights of the Phurnacite Plant at night from my grandmother's bedroom window and thinking how cosy it looked. Everything was cosy there, the terraced houses, the open fires and the people – it was a truly close community. My other grandmother, May Ward, lived at 3 Tanycoed Terrace and when we were walking daily up the hill to visit her and my Uncle David we passed a little shop on the corner, it was like stepping into someone's front room to buy our sweets. I loved my time there, I wish my mother and stepfather had never moved us away, I remember crying every time we left to return down south.

*Pauline Lucas-Milton 109301*

## Halcyon days at Penarth in the 1960s

I remember the excitement of seeing the hovercraft at Penarth as a child. We used to spend many days on the beach at Penarth, usually at the Pier end, but when the hovercraft visited we of course congregated at what we called the 'landing stage' end near the yacht club. This photo shows a boat in the background and I remember a service to Flat Holme that was run by a Mr Noel, or Knowle. We called it 'Knowle's boat'. For many years I craved a journey to Flat Holme on 'Knowle's boat' but never made it. I eventually got there a few years ago, so it only took me 40 years. It was well worth it though. I wonder if anyone else remembers 'Knowle's boat'?

*Michael Evans* 25421

PENARTH, The Hovercraft 1963 P24184

BARRY ISLAND, Whitmore Bay c1960 B29208

## Roller skating at Barry Island

Some of my best memories of Barry Island from the 1960s are from the week-ends I used to go to the skating rink, which was situated above the block of shops on the sea side of the pleasure park overlooking the prom and sea. Three of us waited all week for this wonderful evening. We were me, Pat Baker (I was Pat Overstreet then), Christine Pearce, and Jackie Felix. We all saved hard to buy our own spanking new, white leather roller boots although, impatient to actually wear boots and not simply strap on skates, I bought a secondhand pair from a girl called Roberta who made a wonderful and graceful dance partner with a very handsome young man, Arnold, I seem to remember. We all attempted (and failed) to emulate them! When we did buy our own boots we whitened them before each visit. What a pleasure it was to go home on the 10 past 9 bus (because we had to!) with our skates thrown over our shoulders, tired out, excited, glistening and waiting for the next weekend. Including bus fares and pop, the price for all that fantastic pleasure? 2/6 for the whole evening!

*Patricia Baker 64151*

# What fun we had at Mumbles Pier!

I have many happy memories of Mumbles Pier from the 1950s onwards. It was a place of penny slot machines and there were lots of opportunities to spend your pocket money and have fun! I can remember the Laughing Policeman exhibit – a penny in the slot started an unusual and rather scary model of a Policeman, complete with helmet, swaying from side to side and laughing. There was also the Haunted House where a further penny opened up coffins, cupboards with skeletons and all sorts of ghosts emerging from the spooky house! There were even the naughty machines where we turned handles and which showed 'What The Butler Saw'... where a further few old pennies were used up! Innocent pleasures, but a real treat!

A bag of chips (in newspaper of course), the bracing sea air and the lengthy walk back along the seawall towards Norton made the day complete.

*Gaynor Wingham* *37011*

MUMBLES, The Pier c1965 M108109

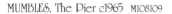

MUMBLES, The Seafront and the Pier c1960 M108078

## Fun at Romilly Park at Barry in the 1960s

Romilly Park not only housed the annual Barry Show, but often the circus, when real animals were allowed! It was great to see the parade coming down Holton Road and making its way to Romilly Park as 'the circus comes to town'.

The Barry Show was altogether different, vegetables, flowers and horses. The best bit was the goodies we were given at the end of the show after doing St John Ambulance first aid duties there. I have fond memories of George Harris and his 3-wheeler Bond together with Frank Johnson who looked after me. *Haydn Ebbs* 72931

# Childhood memories of Glyncorrwg

My memories of Glyncorrwg are from the 1950s to the 1970s. My grandparents lived opposite the Miners' Hall for many years (at 28 Cymmer Road). My grandfather was a bricklayer in the pit and also the Treasurer for the Miners' Hall. I remember leaning on the railings in Cymmer Road with my uncle chatting to the farmer, who lived in the white cottage on the left-hand side approaching the village. I remember sitting on the mountain one summer with my mum, watching the farmer and his wife cutting the hay while my mum and I made baby rattles from the bullrushes. I remember the farmer's white horse who would deliver the milk. I spent every summer holiday in Glyncorrwg. I remember the rain, the sound and smell of the sheep, walking the mountains with my sister, and Sidolli's ice-cream. I remember going to the pictures in the Miners' Hall and in the interval we would go down to Bevan's shop and get an ice-cream. I remember they had entertainment in the Miners' Hall on a Saturday night, and also a library. It was the centre of the community then, apart from the church and chapels of which I believe there were about 9 at one time.

*Beryl Folley* 92931

GLYNCORRWG, The Town 1938 88633

## Our summer holidays at Cwmllynfell

Every year my family would travel to Cwmllynfell for our summer holidays. We went to visit family there (Morgan Morgan of Harris Road). I remember the freedom of playing out, making bows and arrows and exploring. We always had to visit all our close relatives apart from Dadcu. There was Uncle Dai and Aunty Betty, Uncle Will and Aunty Eir who kept a shop, Aunty Gwenny who knew how to do bobbin lace, Uncle Harry and Nesta and Ann who had a small farm on the Bryn, and of course Aunt Hannah, a spinster who lived on the Bryn and managed her house in, what seemed to a young girl, to be strange circumstances... such as putting coal and cement together to make 'Pele'.

*Joyce Morgan* 153831

## Visits to the Cwm

As a child we spent many weekends in Lower Cwmtwrch, near Ystalyfera. My grandparents Horace and Betsy Williams lived there. We spent a lot of time down at the river skipping rocks and cooling off. My grandmother always cleaned the telephone booth across the street from her house – I can still smell the Dettol when I think of it. I have great memories of being there, Dado in his greenhouse taking care of his beautiful flowers, and Mamo carrying buckets of coal into the house for the stove. I remember building a kite and flying it at the top of the hill in a field. We often hopped on the bus to go to Swansea and eat lunch at the Windsor Café.

*Sharon Bondy* 205884

## A Mountain Ash childhood remembered, from the 1970s and 80s

Christmas... ahhh, Christmas. We had no computers or TV games consoles. We had a black and white TV with a rubbish aerial when we reached 11 and a secondhand bike for Christmas from a neighbour who was buying his kids a new one and a snooker table that we had to share with all the street, as you always had a friend if you had a snooker table. There were no fancy stockings with your names on them, we had a rugby sock of my brother's, with white wool at the top for me and a different colour for my siblings. You always knew which had been the Christmas stockings as the first rugby day at school the kids had to play with them around their ankles, as they had all been stretched. If you ever wondered why JPR Williams always played rugby with his socks down to his ankles, now you know.

Halloween was not spent Trick or Treating and knocking doors for money, but spent burning your fingers with candles shoved down swedes if you were rich and empty tins of peas or beans with faces cut out of them with sharp edges you would slice appendages off with if you were poor. We had no make-up on our faces, just the dirt that was always there and added soot from the firelighters we pinched when our candles had long gone.

The Bonfire Nights we spent raiding other local street's bonfires and pinching their wood and rubbish were a real treat. I remember cutting down Silver Birches from the other side of the valley and dragging them across the River Cynon for fear of the police catching us.

Then there was Chapel on a Sunday, also the place for Sunday School, where we all learnt our Christian morals and our songs to sing at night in pubs. We used to sit at the back and send notes and play with Rubik's Cubes, and when the ministers said 'Amen' we were the loudest in the room.

*Clive Francis* 64201

Over 130,000 historic photographs of locations all over Britain can be viewed on the website of The Francis Frith Collection - www.francisfrith.com. The Frith photos were taken between 1860 and 1970, and many website visitors have identified themselves or other family members in some of the views. Here are just a few examples.

## I was there...

Some years ago my mother came across this postcard of Pontycymer and looking carefully saw herself! On the right-hand side of this view, she is the woman, Joan Marion Jones (née Gibson), carrying a child on the corner by what was a barber's. That child is my sister, Christine Jones (now Howell), and the boy beside her is myself. The other lady with her is my Auntie Beat. We were on our way to the railway station in Pontycymer to catch the train to Porthcawl. Christine was born in December 1950 and I was born in November 1947.

*Eric Jones* 39971

PONTYCYMER, Oxford Street c1952 P227008

BRIDGEND, Dunraven Place 1960 B200066

## That's me – going home for lunch!

I am in this photo of Bridgend. I am one of the three girls in Grammar School uniform on the pavement on the left-hand side. The time on the clock in the distance on the right, I believe, is 12.40pm so we must have been going home for lunch. Not many people used to go home from school for lunch but we used to walk together. Hazel Jones (in the middle of the group) was about to cross the road to go over the old stone bridge to Sunnyside Road. But Lorna Jones (on the left) and I used to walk all the way up Newcastle Hill to Cefn Glas. We got plenty of exercise in those days! My name then was Marilyn John. I was 12 years old at the time.

*Marilyn Jones* 40231

## We are the children on the right of this photo...

I believe that the children to the right of the photograph of Tonyrefail are me and my sister - Maureen and Elaine Holman. I (Maureen) would have been 9 years old and Elaine 3 years. The date seems to coincide with our ages and we lived in Mill Street at that time.

*Maureen Harris* 137021

TONYREFAIL, The Square c1955 T156012

## This is my great-grandfather

The gent walking towards the camera on the left-hand side of the road in this view is my great-grandfather and local postman William George Gronow. This is one of the pictures that takes prominence in all my family's homes.

*Nick Thomas* 172151

PORTHCAWL, John Street 1901 47942t

## That's me on my bike!

That's me on the bike in this view, it was 1962, early summer. At that time I was using my step-father's surname of Price. The policeman standing outside the Post Office was Sergeant Brown.

*Bob Powell* 252251

TON PENTRE, Church Road 1962 T191008

## That's my father outside the Post Office

I was born next door to the Post Office at Rhydyfro, which was run by my grandparents David and Mary Jane Phillips. My father, John (Jack Shop) took over the shop when they retired and we moved into the building, which is the larger building, by the telephone post on the right of this view. My father is in the picture standing by the van, which could have been that of a Mr Thomas from Beynamman who supplied the shop with very tasty tomatoes. My father used to supply the surrounding farms with animal food, which was delivered by horse and cart, much to my delight when I accompanied him.

*John Gareth Phillips* 311291

RHYDYFRO, Commercial Road 1938 88364

CHEPSTOW, Disembarking from Beachley Ferry 1950 C77099

## My grandfather is in this view

My grandfather, Reginald Cornish, is standing in front of the car on the slipway (waiting to embark) in the centre of this photo. He was County Engineer for Monmouthshire. I still live in Chepstow and the buildings to the top and left were demolished after the Severn Bridge was built directly above the slip way.

*Roger Cornish* 12511

# I think that's me!

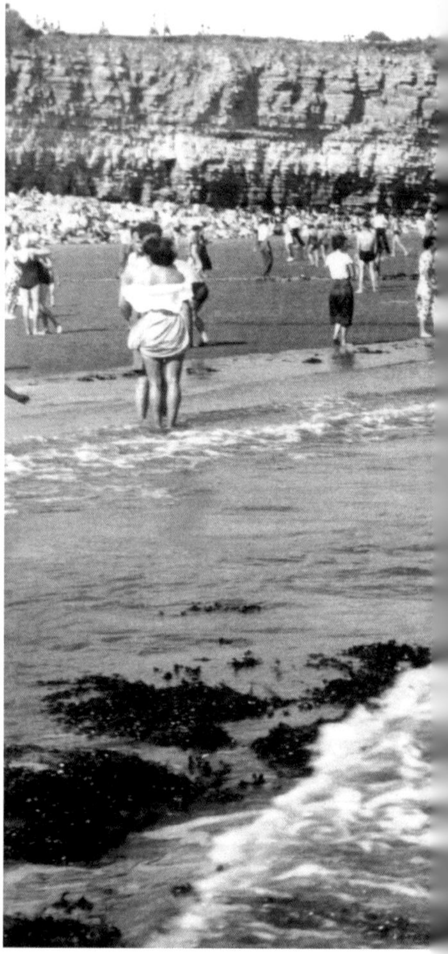

It is quite possible that the little boy to the right in this picture is me at age six. My family used to stay at a friend's caravan in the park above the cliffs. During the summers of 1954 through to 1958 we stayed there most weekends in the summer and even a few in the spring and autumn. St. Mary's Well Bay was not a good beach, there was a lot of rock and bladderwrack seaweed, which does give a satisfying 'pop' when you stand on it. My brothers and I would play for hours along the seashore between Lavernock proper, about a mile to the east, and Swanbridge and Sully Island to the west. On the cliffs above this picture, which is looking north-east, was the 'army camp'. This was a shore battery with large concrete emplacements (sans guns), officers' quarters, and other buildings deserted since the war. The gun batteries were connected by tunnels, probably to move the ordinance, and we had a lot of fun exploring them.

I recall the time as one of great freedom. My mum would let us go and do whatever we wanted, totally unsupervised all day, just coming back for something to eat. Given the enormous tidal reach of the Bristol Channel which would catch and drown a few people each year, the crumbling cliffs, which we climbed with gusto, and the decrepit military camp (now a 'resort'), it is fairly surprising we did not get into some trouble. I am not sure I would allow my six-year-old such freedom, but it was magical at the time.

I revisited the area a few years ago and both the ramp and the steps to the beach have gone, destroyed in a gale. The caravan park is a private resort with a barbed wire fence around it. The beach has even less sand than it used to have, and is even uglier than I remember, but then nobody goes there anyway. The hotel at the top of the ramp burned down many years ago and was not rebuilt. Even the snack shop has gone. People can only get there by driving, as the rail line (steam trains, of course), which used to have daily service between Penarth and Barry, closed a long time ago. The tiny Lavernock station is gone, and I don't even think the track is there any more.

As you can see from the photo, many people used to visit in the 1950s, including one little six-year-old manfully braving the cold waters of the Bristol Channel. But no more.

*Phillip Armour 47811*

LAVERNOCK, St Mary's Well Bay c1955 L279012

*'My mum would let us go and do whatever we wanted, totally unsupervised all day, just coming back for something to eat.'*

## Brynmawr – my hometown

Brynmawr is a quiet little town on the edge of the valley roads. The old photos of the town and surrounding area on the Frith website bring back memories of all the hills I climbed, picnics on the mountain, paddling in the pond across from our house in Warwick Road, and snow 6ft deep in winter. I remember the old steam train passing our house, I would wave to the driver and he would wave back to me as I was standing on a low wooden fence. Everything was at a slow pace in the 1950s. We would go to the local cinema and see mainly Westerns in those days, then come out and get a bag of chips and wander back home, just simple easygoing things. I remember that there were also market stalls inside the picture house, which wouldn't happen now. The market place on a Saturday was something I always loved going to with my grandmother, and seeing the baby chickens and ducks for sale, sometimes buying chickens and carrying them home. I loved those little bundles of yellow fluff – only later to be eating them when they grew.

*Jackie Haynes* 5401/21321

BRYNMAWR, The Valley c1955 B730001

BRYNMAWR, Beaufort Street c1955 B730054

*'Everything was at a slow pace in the 1950s.'*

# Memories of a childhood past, from Risca

My first memory is of being carried by my mother, Bettie, 'Welsh fashion' in a lovely thick shawl, from Constant Row at Risca, where I was born, up the Moriah Hill, over Moriah Bridge and the canal to the quarry, where my Grancha Holder would be sat outside his greenhouse watching the world go by, smoking his pipe – I can still remember the smell of that pipe smoke. Other childhood memories are of running around the quarry playing, chasing the geese, ducks and chickens, and eating the freshly picked tomatoes out of the greenhouse – how sweet they tasted and how wonderful they smelled.

I remember that when he heard the sound of the quarry siren on the other side of the valley at Danygraig before they blasted, my grancha's dog, Laddie, a black mongrel, would gallop up the canal bank past the Prince pub to just past Kears house and he would stand there howling until the siren stopped, then trot off back to my grancha's house on Moriah Hill. This happened every time the siren went off, every day, several times a day. Mental dog!

My days as a child were unlimited happiness, of freedom, playing and wandering wherever and whenever I wanted, no worries in those days. The hilly fields in summer were a favourite with many kids, big and small, we would go armed with cardboard boxes and slide down; it was hard to start with as the grass was still green, but after our endless sliding the grass would brown off, then the sun would do its work to burn it off and after a few days it would be like a glass bottle. We spent hours walking up and sliding down, we must have been the fittest kids in the valleys!

*Jayne Hanks (née Holder)* 28501

RISCA, The Canal Bridge and Moriah Hill c1955 R328306

# Life at Charles Street, Tredegar, in the early decades of the 20th century

My grandma was born Eleanor ('Nellie') Roberts at Back 62 Charles Street at Tredegar on the 27th November 1911; she was the second eldest of 6 girls. She remembers that the cottage had 2 rooms, one up and one down, the upstairs was divided with heavy curtains instead of walls and the girls shared beds. Her dad used to go out with a brown sack up the lanes in Tredegar to collect elderberries to make wine from, when it was brewed he kept the corked bottles under his and the girls' beds in crates, and my grandma remembers every night hearing the corks pop one by one as they fermented!

Grandma was a young girl at school during the First World War and remembers being taken out into the playground to watch a barrage balloon pass over. She went to Nat y Bwch School, I think it's been demolished for many, many years and I believe it was only a small village schoolhouse in the middle of nowhere, but she said there was a sweet shop by it!

As there wasn't a lot to do in those days and they didn't have any money, the children of Tredegar used to walk up to Weavers Farm (I'm not sure if it still exists) nearby on a Saturday morning to watch the slaughterman cut the throat of the pigs. Grandma remembers them running around squealing.

*'One day she and another maid ran away and slept under Tower Bridge until the police found them and took them back.'*

My great-grandfather worked at Grahams Colliery. When my grandma was 12 in 1923 she was told that her dad had died down the pits, found in a puddle of water with a knock on his head. This story carried on until quite recently when I found out that in fact her dad had committed suicide in Cefn Golou Pond because he couldn't go on without any money for the children. I found the original newspaper cutting. It's heartbreaking for us all to know the truth and exactly how hard it was living on his wages with little children. After her dad died, my grandma said that she was very embarrassed at school because it was looked upon as being shameful to not have a father supporting the family. A few months later her mother sent my grandma on her own on a train to London to work in service as a maid in a large white house at the top of Portobello Road. The house belonged to a Jewish tailor who had a workshop on the 3rd floor. Grandma's working hours at the age of 12 were 6am till 11pm daily for 7 years, sending almost all her earnings back to Wales to support her family. One day she and another maid ran away and slept under Tower Bridge until the police found them and took them back. At the time of writing (2008) Grandma is now 96 and still going strong!

*Lee Hutchings* 32991

## I was born at Llanfrechfa Grange Nursing Home, near Cwmbran...

I don't know when it opened as a nursing home nor when it closed, and can find no information of that period, but I was born there in September 1945 at a cost of £3 17s 6d and still have the original invoice! I am proud to have been born in Llanfrechfa.

*Graham Hadley* 132301

## The clanking pipes at the Globe Cinema, Gilfach Goch

I more or less met my late wife, Maureen Purchase as she was then, in the Globe cinema at Gilfach Goch. All the best films were shown there. I remember when King Kong or Tarzan films were shown, there would be a queue all the way up to High Street and down to Johnnie Bacchetа's. I said that we met in the Globe, me and Mo, and we eventually graduated to the double seats in the back row from where we didn't see much of the films. When the weather was cold the central heating would be put on, which would produce a loud clanking in the water pipes every so often, so you were deeply engrossed in a film (sometimes), say a love scene, it would go something like this, the hero would say to his lady love 'I love you darling and I would like to...' – CLANK – CLANK – CLANK, so you would never know what the hero wanted to do. On one side of the building there was an exit door, which opened out onto a covered way. When it was raining, sheep used to shelter there so if you exited by the side door and the light was out, which it was frequently at night, you would be up to your ankles in sheep droppings. Wonderful, wonderful times, I wouldn't change those times for all the free passes to the Workmen's Hall.

*Wyndham Jones* 295081

## Growing up in Croesy

I grew up in Croesyceiliog at Cwmbran, at Raglan Court next to the playing fields, and I went to Abyschan Grammar School. There was no bypass road then, and the railway was still bringing coal from the valleys down to the docks in Newport. I used to lie in bed as a child and hear the train shunting past. In summer when the sun was still high and, though it was bed time, it was too light to sleep, I used to lie in my bed and listen to the sounds of people still up and playing in the fields outside. I remember the woods in spring and the bluebells. My grandmother used to love the bluebells and my siblings and I would pick them for her – mountains of them, of course. My usual childhood troubles were often met by an escape to the woods, and I still can see the sunlight shining through the trees, filtering through the wooded paths I used to know so well.

Australia is home to me now and it's just as beautiful, but my heart will always yearn for the beauty of Cwmbran and the Torfaen.

*Valerie Barton* 156871

## The birth of my Welsh pride

Born at Ebbw Vale in 1952, my memories as a son of a daughter of the valleys are: Rugby - being allowed in for free at half time; trains - lying in bed hearing the clang of the wagons moving coal and steel to and from the works; Armageddon when the furnaces blasted; chasing and riding bare-back on the wild ponies; collecting all the keys from the privies and mixing them up, resulting in a lot of angry desperate people; walking the hills with my uncle, what great country; wind-berry tarts - after nearly sixty years I still hanker after them; the tells of the miners in early graves; the stories of injuries at the steel works; the birth of being proud of my Welsh descent.

*Bob Morgan* 168021

*'Armageddon when the furnaces blasted; chasing and riding bare-back on the wild ponies.'*

EBBW VALE, Market Street c1950 E176004

EBBW VALE, The Steelworks c1960 E176080

EBBW VALE, Mountain Ponies c1960 E176074

## Bath night at Bishton, near Newport, 1945-1950

Unlike today, when my wife and I have 2.5 bathrooms between the two of us and my son has just finished building his second house with three en suite bathrooms, in those days, in mid week, we stood in a metal bowl for a nightly wash, while it was common knowledge that Friday night was bath night. Friday night meant that we lit the fire under the cauldron in the washroom and when the water was hot we ladled it into the slip bath. This wasn't too bad in the gentler seasons but in the winter... I am unsure which of the Bishton houses had bathrooms at that time, now sixty years ago, but metal moveable baths were a staple in many homes at that time.

*Bob Stinchcombe 193391*

## Memories of Aberbeeg

I grew up in Aberbeeg as Pat Howells. Everyone knew the Howells as my dad, Doug, was one of 8 children. My uncle worked in the Webbs Brewery for many years and I grew up in Woodland Terrace and had to pass the brewery at the end of the road every day to go to school. I also remember the old stables on the Square for the brewery dray horses. Dr Edwards had his surgery in the old hay lofts above. I have extremely fond memories of the Switchgear Father Christmas sleigh that used to travel the valleys. Everyone used to brave the cold weather in the Square for a chance to tell him what we wanted for Christmas. I left school in 1970 a year after the brewery had closed. I emigrated to Cape Town in South Africa in 1976 and I relish telling people I meet that I grew up in a street in a small Welsh valley that had a coalmine at the top end (Six Bells Colliery) and a brewery at the bottom. I also had uncles working in the Six Bells Colliery and I remember the disaster in the 1960s that claimed so many lives, God spared my uncles. I was back in Aberbeeg in 2011 and went to see the monument in Six Bells. It was an awe-inspiring and humbling experience to view the list of families who lost loved ones. I am very proud of my Welsh heritage and although I have been in South Africa for a long time, and have become a Springbok rugby supporter, I proudly put on my red Welsh rugby supporter's shirt every time they play Wales.

*Pat Addison 218541*

*'I remember the disaster in the 1960s that claimed so many lives, God spared my uncles.*

## Troedy was the best place in the world to grow up

I was born at Troedrhiwfuwch in 1951 and I lived at 27 High Street next to Doreen's shop, I remember going in for sweets and I could hardly see over the counter and I was always amazed at all the stuff behind it – 'real treasure'. In our house we had a front room which nobody ever used and all the best furniture was in there and I had to walk through there to go upstairs. The toilet was at the top of the garden and was shared with next door. I remember lots of newspapers being in there, and a big wooden seat.

My gran lived near the Post Office. She had gas lamps in the house and we used to make toast on a big brass fork held against the fire. When she made Sunday cooked dinner she got the mint for the sauce from the garden. My two uncles, Ivor and Sammy, lived there and I loved them very much. Ivor would give me fourpence to go down the pub to get a bag of crisps – there was only plain ones then, with a little blue bag of salt inside. Ivor started work down the pit when he was 14 and he died down there when he was 59. Sammy worked the mines all his life too, and when he died he coughed up his lungs.

I've been back to Troedy and there's not much left now. Everything there seems to have shrunk to a smaller size, or is it because I was so small back then? I'm 60 years old now. I remember the swing on the oak tree, and picking wimberries on the mountain, and how the school seemed huge with the bell on top. Troedy was a big place for me back then, and it was the best place to grow up. *John Evans* 257951

## Catching up with the gossip at Troedrhiwfuwch

My mother, Marie Griffiths that was, lived in Troedy until she married in 1952 and moved to the 'Flower'. I remember the bus rides to Troedy to visit my grandmother, Blod. As a young child, I never understood why Mam would get off the bus the other end of Troedy; there was a bus stop closer to my grandmother's house. Years later, I asked her why she did that. Her reply was 'Well, I liked to see all the old neighbours and have a chat'. It used to take us hours before we eventually got to my grandmother's house! I remember her tiny little house; the toilet was at the bottom of the garden, and there was no hot running water and no central heating – but it was in a lovely little community. *Sandra Watkins* 229501

## Troedy was a brilliant place to be...

Well, Troedy certainly keeps its place in people's hearts. It was such a brilliant place to be. I wasn't born there because by the time I came along the men had come back from war and my parents lived in a prefab in Gelligaer. That was a novelty! Our family from Troedy used to come down on the bus, changing in Bargoed, to have their weekly bath. It was tin baths only in Troedy and I remember the ritual well when I visited, which was often. My gran lived in number 20 and two of her brothers lived in the next two houses in the high street. Opposite was her sister and along from there, another brother. I love to remember the way people were in and out of each other's houses or gathered by the railings for a chat. *Ronwen Smith* 344621

# Life in the 1940s at the Charles family home at 39 Cwm Road, Waunlwyd, Ebbw Vale

The Charles family home at 39 Cwm Road at Waunlwyd was on the 'cellar side', which was deemed to be an advantage, since the houses were three-storeyed and sported an extra kitchen, scullery and pantry, not present in those opposite. The front doors of the cellar terrace opened onto the middle floor. From the narrow passage, the doors to the left took you into the parlour and the tiny middle room. At the end of the passage a staircase went up to two little bedrooms. But the hub of the house was DOWN another staircase and through a door immediately at the foot of the stairs, which led into the back kitchen. This wonderful room was home. Mum and Nana Charles were always there, fussing around the old dining table under the window, seeing to the blackleaded range, which was always hungry for illicit coal brought back from the pit by Grandpa Charles. Hours were devoted to filling the tin bath, which served the whole family. Grandpa always had priority treatment in all things, including the bath, and Nana invariably referred to him as 'your poor Grandfather', though I never understood why. My father was given second priority after Grandpa, presumably because he was a married, family man with responsibilities. I can see now that this must have galled my mother's younger and only brother, Wyn, who after all, was the son of the house. Wyn returned from two years in the RAF to find his sister married, and a brother-in-law and niece in residence. Mum talks of those early years with great affection and says she and Dad were never happier, despite a lack of money and space. We officially occupied the parlour and middle room of the house, using the middle room as a bedroom for the three of us, and the parlour as a living room. There was no running water in either room, as Mum always mentions when reminiscing, but my memory is of the whole family using Nana's kitchen, so I don't believe it really mattered. The house, in common with most others in the village, had no inside lavatory, and I was quite used to using a chamberpot at night. The pots were emptied first thing each morning, and I have fond memories of my ladylike grandmother 'emptying the slops'. She would cover the pot with a cloth, and walk through the kitchen, then the scullery, and out to the lavatory at a steady pace and with the expression of a butler engaged in silver service. She must have borne the slops down two flights of stairs, since she and my grandfather slept in one of the rooms on the top floor, whilst Uncle Wyn occupied the other little room.

The pit and the steel works which so dominated life in the valley then provided more than wages and coal. It was also possible to pick up good quality wood no longer needed to prop up the mines. Grandpa and Dad made my potty chair and dolls' house from such gleanings. Grandpa (Norman) Charles worked at the pit, and was on shift work. He was not an easy man and was much affected by the disruption of shifts. His footsteps on the stairs down to the back kitchen instantly changed the atmosphere from cosy chatter to apprehension. He breathed audibly through his teeth, and would emerge into the kitchen with his braces flapping around his knees and one hand grasping his baggy trousers. Usually he continued straight on through the scullery to the lavatory, and was not seen again for some time. Mum and Nana would exchange meaningful glances, and the chatter would resume.

*Raye Green* 332741

## My grandmother always had the front door open...

I was brought up in Jamesville at Cwmcarn in the Ebbw Valley. My family lived in the same house from 1911 until 2011 when my father passed away at 90. There are very few of the old families still there. By old I mean the families that were friendly with my grandmother who moved there in 1911 when the children married. The usual thing then, when children got married, was to move within the same street near their mum and dad!

Memories...When I grew up my grandmother always had the front door open, whatever the weather, so it seemed to me – if the door was closed, neighbours would knock to see what was wrong. Doors never seemed to be locked. Parents, sons and daughters would be living fairly close to one another, so there were several homes in the street with related families. That was fairly common in those days for all streets. I remember when the street was not tarmacked, we used to be able to select stones for our catapults from the street and go off to the canal with heavy pockets. The local streets must have been tarmacked about 1958-ish. *Brian Downes 272041*

*'When I grew up my grandmother always had the front door open, whatever the weather, so it seemed to me – if the door was closed, neighbours would knock to see what was wrong.'*

## Living in Cefn Hengoed

The Kemp family lived in Cefn Hengoed from about 1920 to 1938. I was born there in my grandparents' house (James and Rose Kemp), number 64 Gelligaer Road, in 1934. My memories of the village start from about 1937. I remember seeing a bus go flashing by down Gelligaer Road with its interior lights on. When I questioned my dad, Thomas John Kemp (also known as Jack), he said it was the St John's Ambulance Brigade's bus going to a disaster, some workmen had been erecting an electricity pylon nearby which had collapsed, and they were going to help. He and my Uncle Jim were very involved with the St John's Ambulance Brigade in the village and I suppose he was on the bus. Another memory of life in the village is of playing in the field at the top of the village near the Cross-Keys pub, whilst waiting for my dad to come out of the pub, my elder brother Harry and I were playing on the wall and Harry fell in the manure. My last memory of the village is of leaving on the furniture van and the journey up to Nuneaton in 1938 after my grandparents James and Rose Kemp had died, we (Mam, Harry, Marge and I) sat in the back of the van on the settee. *Jack Kemp 41371*

## Life at River Row, Treherbert, in the 1950s

My family lived in the end cottage in River Row at Treherbert, our garden backed on to the river and railway line beyond. My brother and I were aged 3 and 4 years old and I can remember waving to my father as he went to work in the pits, the train was a bit far away but my dad used to wave a white handkerchief at us. My brother fell in the river once and nearly drowned, he was about 5 years old and I was 4 years old, I lay down on my tummy on a water pipe and pulled him out. We went home soaking wet and our dad told us off, our mum was at the pictures - they used to take it in turn to go to the pictures. Another time we followed the marching band all the way to Blaenrhondda Park, sitting on the kerbside every time the band stopped for a break.

*Patricia Greenacre* 112221

TREHERBERT, Station Road c1955 T196001

## Blaenllechau, in the Rhondda Fach valley – my childhood home

I was brought up in Blaenllechau, immediately after the Second World War, when life was not as complicated as it is today. Our playground included all the mountain behind us, Llanwonno, the woods and even the park. I delivered papers around the village and the majority of houses did not have locks on, it was open the door, drop the paper in and close it.

*Brian Evans 150411*

> *'Our playground included all the mountain behind us, Llanwonno, the woods and even the park.'*

## What went on at Caerau Library in the 1960s besides reading…

I lived both at Church Street, Caerau and at Lloyd Street, Caerau, the latter being close to the library. Often as young people we would play snooker and table tennis at the library, sometimes even read the newspapers there. Girls were never allowed in, and the place was always filled with smoke, for all the men that played on the tables would be smoking their fags.

*David Walters 173441*

> *'Girls were never allowed in, and the place was always filled with smoke.'*

## We lived in one of these houses when they were new

This photograph shows the newly built council houses at Gilfach Goch called Danybryn. The houses were much sought after by the mining community as they had bathrooms. My parents lived in number 5 and thought their house was wonderful even though the rent was expensive for the time, £1.15 shillings a week.

*'My parents lived in number 5 and thought their house was wonderful.'*

GILFACH GOCH, Danybryn c1955 G177029

PONTYPRIDD, Taff Street 1952 P716007

## Memories of the Graig district of Ponypridd, from the 1940s and 50s

I was born in the house of Williams the Milk on the corner of Graig Avenue; my over-riding memories of the following few years are mainly of the horse and cart Mr Williams used, pulled by his horse 'Dolly'. I sometimes went on the milk round with them, travelling through the Graig, Treforest, Merthyr Road, to Trallwn, and finally through Taff Street. At the Tumble Mr Williams would get Dolly up to a gallop to cross the square and pass under the railway bridge to make a left turn into Union Street; it was often touch-and-go whether Dolly would make it up the steep hill and round the corner. I went to a school in Maesycoed and remember going to bed in the afternoons. There was a small bakery near the school and to this day the smell of fresh bread triggers of memories of those years.

*John Davies 205105*

NANTYMOEL c1955 N121014

## How we lived at Nantymoel

1947 was the year my parents, sister aged 4 and myself aged 10 moved from living in two rooms in a shared house in Pricetown to a rundown three-storeyed rented house in Llewellyn Street, Nantymoel. It had three bedrooms, without electricity on the top floor, two living rooms and a pantry on the middle floor with electricity which was accessed by the front door from street level; below ground under the pavement was a coal cellar and another pantry which opened onto a further unusable living room with a back door onto the garden. Immediately outside the back door was a toilet, a wooden bench 2ft 6ins wide with a hole. It emptied into a sewer but had no flush, you just emptied a bucket of water down it after it was used. The only water tap in the house was a standpipe just inside the back door, so at least you didn't have far to carry the heavy zinc bucket. A zinc bath hung on the outside wall. It was carried up to the first floor every Friday evening, then began the filling of it. The hot water was supplied from the reservoir at the side of the fire, the other side of the fire was an oven. Cold water was carried up via a ladder-type stairs (treads which overlapped). After my mother, sister and I had used it (Dad bathed at the colliery), the water was carried out a bucketful at a time and thrown down the gutter drain outside the front door. Yet we thought we were in heaven because we had the whole house to ourselves. The front and back doors had latches and no locks, so the only time the house was secured was at night when you shot the bolts before going to bed. Llewellyn Street is the third row of houses in the foreground of this picture.

*Margaret Davies* 11251

## The whole of Caerau knew who she was!

George Street at Caerau, what a wonderful happy street to live in. My Aunt Mable, Terry my cousin and my wonderful granma lived at number 30 for many years. I would be there whenever I could, I always called George Street home, it was really. Anyway, back in 1964, I was bringing my wife-to-be to see Caerau. I wrote a letter (there were no telephones or mobiles then) to Aunt Mable, saying when we would be down. I had to work all day on the Friday so didn't leave Cambridge until early evening. Of course, there were no motorways then so it was a long drive across country. We arrived late Friday night, about midnight I think. In the morning, I slept in, my wife-to-be Janet knew I was out of cigarettes so she walked down to the Square to get some for me. (I don't smoke now, it's a mug's game.) I got up about 10am, and Janet was upset, why?

It appears that as she walked to the Square and back, most people spoke to her, talking to her by her name. Of course she never spoke to anybody, as a city girl she was not used to people being friendly. I just laughed, and said 'Of course everybody knew you, and who you are'. Mable had told next door that Colin was coming home and bringing his bride-to-be, and within an hour all of George Street knew, and by the time we got there, about three weeks later, most people in Caerau knew. Janet was a stranger in the village, so two and two made four!

I will always hold George Street close to my heart, both the street and the people.

*Colin Cornwell 86101*

*'Mable had told next door that Colin was coming home and bringing his bride-to-be, and within an hour all of George Street knew.'*

## Full coal sheds at Blackmill, near Gilfach Goch...

I wonder how many people remember the coal train, with all its trucks full of coal, breaking down on the Gilfach line behind Isfryn prefabs at Blackmill; it was there all night and plenty of people had full coal sheds by morning!

*David Diamond 335661*

# Cissie's Memories of Barry in the early 1900s

I came to Barry in 1900. Holton Road was muddy then and planks of wood were put down to enter the shops. We had a shop in 26 Holton Road, and later at the bottom of the block on spare ground Johnson's opened a portable theatre. They played drama and had a pantomime in which I took part as a chorus girl. On the other side of the road was a family called Langley. They lived in a caravan and had swings and a coconut shy.

Mr Jones had an undertaker's shop in Holton Road and there was Mr John the butcher, Hicks the chemist, Folicks the pawnbroker, Tibbets the grocer and Maypole grocers shop. Horses and carts were used then, and later on Whites ran a bus (open top) to the Island for 3d return. Later on a theatre was built in the field next to the old brewery, and on Priory Hill a monastery was built of corrugated iron and monks lived there. The building is still there and is now the Four Lanterns Inn.

I can remember going over to Barry Island with my stepfather and mother to see the bonfire and roasting of the ox to celebrate the Relief of Mafeking on 24th May 1900, during the Boer War.

The docks were always full of ships, and there were plenty of foreign people about the town from them.

*Submitted to the Frith website on Cissie's behalf by Linda* 69511

BARRY, Holton Road 1903 50851

BARRY, The Docks 1899 43451

## Joseph Williams – Joe Bach – of Ystalyfera

Joseph Williams was my great-grandfather who lived at Tirbach Road, Ystalyfera. During his life he had much bad fortune. He lost a leg in an accident, his wife died at a young age and a daughter was drowned in the canal. According to a person who wrote for the local paper at the time of his death in 1933, in spite of all he maintained a bright outlook on life. 'Alltygrug' in a tribute to Joe Bach tells a story of him digging for coal behind his house, when a friend told him to 'come out' before a fall came. He declined and a fall buried him up to his shoulders. Prompt steps were taken to free him and meanwhile he maintained his cheerfulness, his only concern being for his artificial limb: 'Mind my leg', he implored his rescuers. He and his white horse pulling a cart carrying coal were a well-known sight in Ystayfera in the late 1920s and early 1930s. 'Alltygrug' notes on his death in 1933: 'His horse and cart – frequently an interesting study in black and white – will be absent from our street and we cannot replace him. A new era is with us.'

*David Thomas 138381*

## The good old days at Loughor, near Swansea

I remember buying sweets from the sweet shop you can just see the entrance to the shop behind the car in this photograph, you could buy a lot for 3 pence then (in the late 1950s). If I remember correctly there was a fish and chip shop around the corner where we bought our fish and chips, they were wrapped up in newspaper, they never tasted better. We used to take our old newspapers down to the shop, they always needed newspaper. Nothing happened to us from eating fish and chips out of newspaper, I'm 64 now.

*Robert Coleman 255891*

LOUGHOR, The Cross c1960 L466017

## Steamed pasties to die for at Belli's Café, Blaenavon

This photo looking down Broad Street at Blaenavon was taken c1955, five years before I was born. My name is Stephen Belli and I was adopted by the Belli family in 1963. I lived in the town until 1990. I particularly remember the hot summer of 1976 – I was 16 and studying for my O levels in between minding the shop for my adopted parents, Bert and Mary Belli. Our café was one of two Belli Cafés in the town, but of course I always thought ours was superior and served the best steamed pasties and pies. The pasties were to die for. If Phillip Pritchard whose parents owned the old Spar shop is still about, I recall him eating 3 or 4 before his Sunday dinner! I have fond memories of the kids coming into the shop and playing music on the old juke box and seeing if they could beat my score on the flipper machine. Of course I had an unfair advantage because my Uncle Bert had the key. We also made the best ice-cream in town. I spent many long hours serving ice-cream in the shop – raspberry ripple seemed to be the favourite.

That summer of 1976 was also eventful because of the huge mountain fire on the Blorenge. The peat caught fire and it took the local fire brigade many weeks to bring it under control. I remember having to keep the doors and windows shut to keep out the pall of smoke hanging over the town. *Stephen Belli 73941/20201*

BLAENAVON, Broad Street c1955 B672014

## Our customers remember Belli's Café...

We run a Welsh gift shop in the premises that was previously Belli's Café at Blaenavon, most days we have customers reminiscing about how they did their 'courting' in Belli's. There are also lots of fond memories of steamed pasties, but my favourite are the stories from men who, when they were boys and misbehaved in the café, received a swift clip around the ear, or the wrong end of a dishcloth. Those were the days! *Gary Mills 73281*

# Telephoning and selling sweets at Risca in the 1950s

The public telephone in this picture of Tredegar Street at Risca was outside my father's butcher shop. There were only two buttons to press, button A and button B, but people were terrified of pressing the wrong one, so my father, Gomer Mumford, used to do the phoning for lots of people. Sometimes coins would jam in the mechanism so he would release them using a butcher's knife and pocket the money!

Next door to the butcher shop, my mother Adelaide opened a flower shop just before the Coronation of Queen Elizabeth II in 1953. Bit by bit we added plants, fruit and vegetables. When sweets came off ration we also sold confectionery. Such was the pent-up craving for sweets that I remember selling fifteen 7lb jars of Sherbert Lemons in a day. People queuing for the Palace cinema used to buy sweets and cigarettes from us. All the family would be on hand to cope with the tremendous rush of trade. We had a side window devoted to sweets for children. At lunchtime we would be pressed to the wall as we counted out Aniseed Balls and Blackjacks. Liquorice Rolls and Sherbert Fountains were also popular items.

*Cedric Mumford 77461*

RISCA, Tredegar Street c1955 R328017

# Kibby Grocers and other memories of Aberbeeg

My grandfather was Harry Kibby the Stores, Aberbeeg Bakers & Grocers. I remember visiting as a child every Saturday and sweeping the yard, my reward was a bottle of Coca Cola, unknown in those days. I collected my 'Beano' from Lou Poole's shop over the little bridge and got a haircut at Mr Jones the Barber where there was a little window to check who was waiting. I remember the Carnival in 1953 and the crowning of the May Queen. I also had a job taking slices of oranges over the bridge to the football field for the players, hoping that they might leave one for me. My uncles Arthur and Harry junior played football and rugby for Aberbeeg.

*Glyn Davies 82391*

# I remember these shops at Waunlwyd

I was born in 1955 and lived in Waunlwyd until I went away to University in 1973. I remember this row of shops very well as I was entrusted to shop for family and relatives who would pay me a small fee that I was saving up for a school trip to Paris (that never took place). I remember Mr and Mrs Morgan in the Post Office – who I think you can see in the photo – with their Corgi dog. Mr Morgan told the corniest jokes in the world but it was always a treat to go in there. Next door was John Rogers the butchers and I can remember the older Mr Rogers gutting a chicken while carrying on a conversation with a customer – I was about 8 at the time and found it shocking. Next door was Bessie Smith the greengrocers and next to that was a shop with two entrances, one to a hairdressers and the other to a wool/knitting patterns and haberdashery shop. This was owned or run by Betty Manship, I think. The shop next door became a chip shop and, when I was a little bit older, we used to congregate in the back room where they had a pinball machine. The owner was Peter Angwin who was very patient with us as we didn't buy too many chips. I may have missed out a shop from this row but this photo brought back a torrent of memories.

*Chris Hodson 141741*

WAUNLWYND, The Parade, Park Place c1955 W470007

# My memories of Pontypool town centre in the 1960s

I lived in Upper Bridge Street at Pontypool and remember a few of the shops in town, I think! The market was full of country people with veg stalls on a Saturday, and my particular favourite was the Trumans' sweet stall with their fabulous hardboiled sweets called Emma's that were made in a tiny factory in Lower Bridge Street. Mrs Truman was very glamorous and her husband very handsome - their sister Kitty was a staunch member of St James Church choir. The large fruiterer's at the bottom was called 'Under the Clock' because it was, and at the top end was a wet fish stall whose name I've forgotten. Opposite was Sidoli's chip shop and further down was the Octagon library where my nan bought me colouring and reading books. Next door was a dry cleaner's with a lady sat at a machine in the window making invisible repairs to nylon stockings. Opposite was Daniel's the grocers with a fabulous smell inside, later discovered to be freshly ground coffee beans - we still had Camp coffee at home. At the bottom, Fowler's was on the one corner with Commercial Street and Pegler's grocers in the other. Opposite, on the Cross, was Winterhalter's jeweller's shop and further along, towards George Street, was the Home & Colonial grocer's where my mum worked before she married. I remember sugar packed in blue bags with neat folds at the top, Nizzam tea, big metal boxes with glass lids for biscuits that were bought by the pound, and slabs of butter in greaseproof paper. And not forgetting Woolworth's where I worked on Saturdays despite being censored by my Headmistress at school.

*Sandra Rudd (née Waters)* 388041

PONTYPOOL, George Street c1960 P126034

## Who remembers Stuchbery's at Bridgend?

Who remembers Stuchbery's at Bridgend – the first shop on the left in this photograph? It was an Aladdin's cave. My mum used to buy dress fabric and haberdashery there. Do you remember the vacuum tubes that took the money to the cashier and then came back with your receipt and your change? They used to fascinate me when I was little. We had to go there for most of the Girls' Grammar School uniform – the rest you had to get in Evans the Outfitters in Cardiff.

*Elizabeth Roberts (née Trevelyan) 72521*

BRIDGEND, Caroline Street c1965 B200112

## I do!

The Stuchbery's shop in Caroline Street at Bridgend was owned by my grandfather and his brother, and like Elizabeth Roberts in her memory (above), I too was fascinated by the tubes which carried cash to the office at the back of the shop. During visits to the shop with Granny I can remember at a very young age trying to jump on the foot pedal with enough force to send the little cartridges back out into the shop. I have fond memories of my grandfather who was a small bald gentleman – he cycled into the shop about 2 miles each day from his home well into his sixties.

*Paul Bygrave 106251*

## My great-grandmother cleaned City Hall in the early 20th century

My mother was from Newtown in Cardiff, near the docks. It was a community of very poor Irish immigrants. My great-grandmother had a job cleaning the City Hall. She would walk through Cardiff in the early morning and do her work which included polishing the steps then walk all the way back home again, a good few miles. On the way she would stop at her friend's house and her friend would make her a cup of tea, her first sustenance of the day. I am proud of my hard-working forbears. My grandmother could barely write her name, but I've had the privilege of attending three Universities, because they valued education and learning.

*Marian Foot* 386271

CARDIFF, City Hall, Law Courts 1906 54941

## My Uncle Douglas Webber

My grandparents lived in Cardiff Street, Ogmore Vale. My grandfather and uncle both worked in the mine. Sometime in the late 1930s there was an accident and everyone got out, but my uncle who was an animal lover went back to save his horse and got killed, the horse got out safe. My grandmother was cleaning her front step when someone came and told her of the death. She never got over the death and never spoke of it.

*Theresa Sinnick* 202947

## My father worked at the Marine Colliery at Cwm

My father worked at the Marine Colliery at Cwm for over 20 years. His name was Jack Bedford, from Brynmawr, a hard working man. There was a pitfall in 1964 where a friend and workmate was killed, and he brought this poor man to the surface. I remember him coming home crying. I had never seen him cry before. Those miners worked in awful conditions, up past their knees in water, with a pick and shovel. I'm always going to be proud of my dad, and what he done for his kids. I remember one time he had a beat knee, where his knee was just rotting from standing in dirty water for hours. He died in 1995 – God bless you, my beautiful dad.

*Jackie Haynes 5121*

CWM, The Marine Colliery c1960 C517037

## Kneeling in water to collect the coal...

Jackie Haynes's father Jack Bedford who she mentions in her memory (above) was known to us, his workmates, as Jackie Bedford. I worked with him on the B7 Black Vein seam where the roof fall occurred. The 'fall' killed two men, Jack Timothy and Idris Paul, two lives snuffed out by a (in my opinion) basic mining engineering error. My father worked on that coalface as well, he was 'Ike Pidgeon' (his proper name was Ivor Williams). Jackie Haynes is spot on in her comments about our working conditions, there was roof water like a continuous heavy rainfall, pouring down your neck and running out of the lace-holes of your boots. Your workwear, including your underwear, was sodden the whole of the shift. The seam was just over a metre high on B6 so it meant that you had to kneel in a foot of water to work the coal, all day, with freezing cold water swilling about your thighs. I remember Jackie Bedford and I'll never forget that hell-hole called Black Vein B7. Yes, most of us cried that day, thinking, selfishly perhaps, there but for the grace of God go I. *David Williams 245181*

## Swimming after our shift at Mountain Ash

I worked in Deep Duffryn Pit at Mountain Ash. After working a night shift we'd sometimes go straight to the swimming pool at 07.30am. Often we'd have to wait for the pool attendant, Mr Prosser, to skim the dust from the top of the water, then we'd go in. Cold, yes, but only at first. Happy days.

*Brian James* 231311

MOUNTAIN ASH, The Swimming Baths c1955 M175034

## A mining community gone without a trace at Treodrhiwfuwch

When they first found coal, Treodrhiwfuwch was only a farm. Over the years terraced houses were built for the miners, some turned into shops. My father, David Thomas Harris, was born 16th Feb 1917 in one of those houses. He went to school there and at the age of ten he was awarded a silver medal for three years never having a day off. At fourteen he, like so many before him, went down the pits, a dirty, dangerous job but that was all there was for work. He stayed down the pits for 10 back-breaking years. When the Second World War broke out he joined up to leave the pits behind. When the coal pinched out the whole community vanished, including the houses – gone without a trace. My father died at the age of 93, but he is not gone without a trace. He is in our hearts, as is Tredrhiwfuwch.

*David Harris* 161671

# Working at Senghennydd Railway Station in the 1950s

At 17 years of age, after interviews at British Railways' commercial HQ at Cymric Buildings in Cardiff, I started work as a Booking Clerk at Senghennydd Station. I lived in Bargoed, travelling each day to Senghennydd via Caerphilly to start work at 6am. Mr Hugh E Williams was the Station Master, Jack Jones and Bill Manship were both Porters. Glyn Williams and Jim Moss were both Signalmen in the tiny signal box by the little bridge at the end of the platform. Trains comprised of only 2 carriages and as the station was at the top end of the Aber valley, the engine had to be uncoupled and transferred to what was the last carriage for the return journey to Cardiff. Occasionally, in summer, we had trains of 5 or 7 coaches to cater for Chapel or Club outings to Barry Island. Normally Senghennydd received about 8 trains each day, miners travelled the short distance to the Windsor Colliery, other passengers travelled to schools in Caerphilly or work at Sherman's Pools and shops in Cardiff. Most purchased weekly or monthly season tickets. Early morning return tickets to Windsor Colliery cost 6 pence (2.5p in decimal money), a day return to Cardiff Queen Street cost 2 shillings and 9 pence (approximately 14p now), or after 4pm it cost 1 shilling and 6 pence (7.5p). Average takings each day at the station amounted to £6. On Mondays the total would rise to about £20, when weekly tickets were purchased. Early trains brought a varying selection of parcels, mainly mail order items for residents and perishable items for local shops. All had to be delivered by the Porter on early shift using a heavy 2-wheeled hand-cart, with cursing by Porter Jack Jones if some deliveries were to addresses higher up in the town.

Mr Hugh Williams, the Station Master, a very heavy smoker, also ran a newsagent's shop in the town which, I think, was previously called Mary Thomas's. He used to vanish for about 2 hours to sort and sometimes deliver papers in the morning and for much longer periods in the afternoon to help his son in the running of the shop, leaving me, as a 17-year-old boy, to run the station office, which made me feel very important but bored stiff. However, it gave me the opportunity to use the telephone for private calls, especially to my aunty in London. The station telephone number was Senghennydd 69 and it was a 'candlestick model' telephone. Abertridwr was Aber 29, where the Station Master was Mr Percy Price. Both Station Masters were forever at each other's throat over trivialities or seniority which I found very amusing in adults holding such (as was regarded in those days) important positions.

Other than holiday times with luggage sent in advance, we were not very busy with outgoing parcel traffic, except those very heavy parcels containing metal components manufactured by Morfed Products Ltd which, by their weight, provided a good source of revenue each day. Each day's takings had to be locked in a leather pouch bearing the station name and deposited into a travelling safe on a mid morning train. The safe was a large square strong box with a mechanism similar to a Bank night safe. This was the method used throughout the valleys stations in those days and only Station Masters were authorised to deposit into these safes, overlooked by the Guard. Somewhere in Cardiff the bags were retrieved, but I remember that on one occasion our bag was returned with the previous day's takings inside. This was kept very quiet when Head Office was advised. I recently visited Senghennydd but found no trace of the station or goods yard, but fond memories remain.

*Arthur Davies 228901*

## I worked at the Semtex factory at Brynmawr

I worked in the Semtex factory for six months in 1962 as part of a management training programme with Dunlop. The work was mainly the production of vinyl asbestos tiles but there was a unit for making rubber underlay. This was a hell-hole where ammonia fumes were rife. For a while there was an attempt at diversification in producing fibreglass rod blanks, suitable for fishing rods. It was a friendly place and I had lodgings with Alf and Doris Sillman, a lovely couple.

Geoff Brickell was the Export Manager, with a hobby of wood turning. I still have a bowl he made. The factory had a very good male voice choir. I don't think any of them could read music but they had the Welsh innate sense of harmony. There were two top tenors in particular with that special quality you find in the valleys.

While the factory was noted architecturally, the architect had an innovative idea for a spiral staircase – to make it self-standing, without a central post. The result was that it turned into a giant spring. As you walked up or down it the whole thing bounced!

*David Osborne* 222611

BRYNMAWR, Semtex Factory c1965 B730103

## My grandfather was the head gardener there

I was so pleased to find the photos of the gardens at the Welsh Folk Museum at St Fagans on the Frith website, as there don't seem to be very many around. My grandfather Trevor Dimond was the head gardener there. He started just after the war and was there for 30 years and boy, did he and his men work hard, starting at 6.00am and finishing at 10.00pm to maintain the standards. I lived with him and my grandmother in The Gardens House, a large house tucked away in the museum, now unfortunately offices, and my playground as a child was the gardens, it couldn't have been more magical.

I am so proud of the work my grandfather put into the gardens and often visit and look back. I remember him nurturing the seedlings to plant on when the season was right, pruning the red and black vines of the grapes in the greenhouses that visitors used to buy, and the smell of the flowers on summer evenings. I really wish there was more of his work shown in the museum today but he was never one to get photographed or interviewed too much, he would be quietly in the background. I have had a bench dedicated to him that overlooks the ponds, on the other side of the castle, so should you ever sit down for a rest and take in the beauty of the gardens, spare a thought for the great, hard working man that got it all going from virtually nothing.

*John Brewer* *72001*

ST FAGANS, The Formal Gardens, Welsh Folk Museum c1960 S16007

# Francis Frith

## Pioneer Victorian Photographer

Francis Frith, founder of the world-famous photographic archive, was a multi-talented man. A devout Quaker and a highly successful Victorian businessman, he was philosophical by nature and pioneering in outlook. By 1855 he had already established a wholesale grocery business in Liverpool, and sold it for the astonishing sum of £200,000, which is the equivalent today of over £15,000,000. Now in his thirties, and captivated by the new science of photography, Frith set out on a series of pioneering journeys up the Nile and to the Near East.

He was the first photographer to venture beyond the sixth cataract of the Nile. Africa was still the mysterious 'Dark Continent', and Stanley and Livingstone's historic meeting was a decade into the future. The conditions for picture taking confound belief. He laboured for hours in his wicker dark-room in the sweltering heat of the desert, while the volatile chemicals fizzed dangerously in their trays. Back in London he exhibited his photographs and was 'rapturously cheered' by members of the Royal Society. His reputation as a photographer was made overnight.

By the 1870s the railways had threaded their way across the country, and Bank Holidays and half-day Saturdays had been made obligatory by Act of Parliament. All of a sudden the working man and his family were able to enjoy days out, take holidays, and see a little more of the world.

With typical business acumen, Francis Frith foresaw that these new tourists would enjoy having souvenirs to commemorate their days out. For the next thirty years he travelled the country by train and by pony and trap, producing fine photographs of seaside resorts and beauty spots that were keenly bought by millions of Victorians. These prints were painstakingly pasted into family albums and pored over during the dark nights of winter, rekindling precious memories of summer excursions. Frith's studio was soon supplying retail shops all over the country, and by 1890 F Frith & Co had become the greatest specialist photographic publishing company in the world, with over 2,000 sales outlets, and pioneered the picture postcard.

Francis Frith had died in 1898 at his villa in Cannes, his great project still growing. By 1970 the archive he created contained over a third of a million pictures showing 7,000 British towns and villages.

Frith's legacy to us today is of immense significance and value, for the magnificent archive of evocative photographs he created provides a unique record of change in the cities, towns and villages throughout Britain over a century and more. Frith and his fellow studio photographers revisited locations many times down the years to update their views, compiling for us an enthralling and colourful pageant of British life and character.

We are fortunate that Frith was dedicated to recording the minutiae of everyday life. For it is this sheer wealth of visual data, the painstaking chronicle of changes in dress, transport, street layouts, buildings, housing and landscape that captivates us so much today, offering us a powerful link with the past and with the lives of our ancestors.

Computers have now made it possible for Frith's many thousands of images to be accessed almost instantly. The archive offers every one of us an opportunity to examine the places where we and our families have lived and worked down the years. Its images, depicting our shared past, are now bringing pleasure and enlightenment to millions around the world a century and more after his death. For further information visit: www.francisfrith.com

# Index of Photographs

# FRITH PRODUCTS & SERVICES

Francis Frith would doubtless be pleased to know that the pioneering publishing venture he started in 1860 still continues today. Over a hundred and forty years later, The Francis Frith Collection continues in the same innovative tradition and is now one of the foremost publishers of vintage photographs in the world. Some of the current activities include:

## INTERIOR DECORATION

Today Frith's photographs can be seen framed and as giant wall murals in thousands of pubs, restaurants, hotels, banks, retail stores and other public buildings throughout the country. In every case they enhance the unique local atmosphere of the places they depict and provide reminders of gentler days in an increasingly busy and frenetic world.

## PRODUCT PROMOTIONS

Frith products are used by many major companies to promote the sales of their own products or to reinforce their own history and heritage. Frith promotions have been used by Hovis bread, Courage beers, Scots Porage Oats, Colman's mustard, Cadbury's foods, Mellow Birds coffee, Dunhill pipe tobacco, Guinness, and Bulmer's Cider.

## GENEALOGY AND FAMILY HISTORY

As the interest in family history and roots grows world-wide, more and more people are turning to Frith's photographs of Great Britain for images of the towns, villages and streets where their ancestors lived; and, of course, photographs of the churches and chapels where their ancestors were christened, married and buried are an essential part of every genealogy tree and family album.

## FRITH PRODUCTS

All Frith photographs are available Framed or just as Mounted Prints and unmounted versions. These may be ordered from the address below. Other products available are - Calendars, Jigsaws, Canvas Prints, Mugs, Tea Towels, Tableware and local and prestige books.

## THE INTERNET

Over several hundred thousand Frith photographs can be viewed and purchased on the internet through the Frith websites!

For more detailed information on Frith products, look at www.francisfrith.com

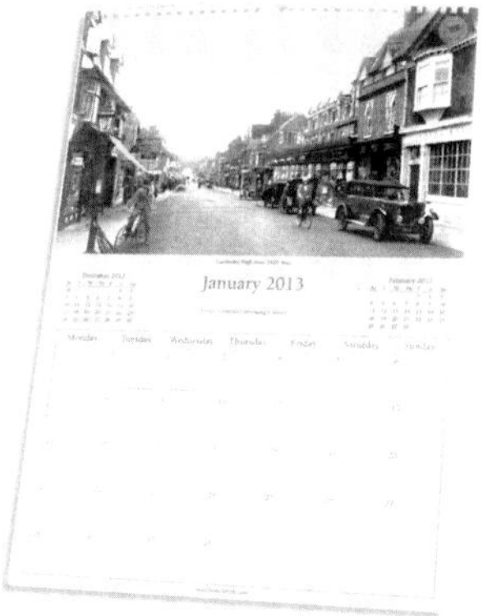


**See the complete list of Frith Books at: www.francisfrith.com**
This web site is regularly updated with the latest list of publications from The Francis Frith Collection. If you wish to buy books relating to another part of the country that your local bookshop does not stock, you may purchase on-line.

***For further information, trade, or author enquiries please contact us at the address below:***
**The Francis Frith Collection, 19 Kingsmead Business Park, Gillingham, Dorset SP8 5FB.**
Tel: +44 (0)1722 716 376 Email: sales@francisfrith.co.uk

See Frith products on the internet at www.francisfrith.com

# FREE PRINT OF YOUR CHOICE

## CHOOSE A PHOTOGRAPH FROM THIS BOOK

+ POSTAGE

**Mounted Print**

*Overall size 14 x 11 inches (355 x 280mm)*

### TO RECEIVE YOUR FREE PRINT

**Choose any Frith photograph in this book**

Simply complete the Voucher opposite and return it with your remittance for £3.80 (to cover postage and handling) and we will print the photograph of your choice in SEPIA (size 11 x 8 inches) and supply it in a cream mount ready to frame (overall size 14 x 11 inches).

**Order additional Mounted Prints at HALF PRICE - £19.00 each** (normally £38.00)

If you would like to order more Frith prints from this book, possibly as gifts for friends and family, you can buy them at half price (with no additional postage costs).

**Have your Mounted Prints framed**

For an extra £20.00 per print you can have your mounted print(s) framed in an elegant polished wood and gilt moulding, overall size 16 x 13 inches (no additional postage required).

**IMPORTANT!**

❶ Please note: aerial photographs and photographs with a reference number starting with a "Z" are not Frith photographs and cannot be supplied under this offer.

❷ Offer valid for delivery to one UK address only.

❸ These special prices are only available if you use this form to order. You must use the ORIGINAL VOUCHER on this page (no copies permitted). We can only despatch to one UK address.

❹ This offer cannot be combined with any other offer.

As a customer your name & address will be stored by Frith but not sold or rented to third parties. Your data will be used for the purpose of this promotion only.

*Send completed Voucher form to:*

**The Francis Frith Collection, 19 Kingsmead Business Park, Gillingham, Dorset SP8 5FB**

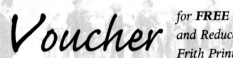

# *Voucher* *for FREE and Reduced Price Frith Prints*

*Please do not photocopy this voucher. Only the original is valid, so please fill it in, cut it out and return it to us with your order.*

| Picture ref no | Page no | Qty | Mounted @ £19.00 | Framed + £20.00 | Total Cost £ |
|---|---|---|---|---|---|
| | | 1 | Free of charge* | £ | £ |
| | | | £19.00 | £ | £ |
| | | | £19.00 | £ | £ |
| | | | £19.00 | £ | £ |
| | | | £19.00 | £ | £ |
| | | | £19.00 | £ | £ |
| | | | * Post & handling | | £3.80 |
| | | | **Total Order Cost** | | £ |

*Please allow 28 days for delivery. Offer available to one UK address only*

Title of this book ................................

I enclose a cheque/postal order for £ ...........

made payable to 'The Francis Frith Collection'

OR please debit my Mastercard / Visa / Maestro card, details below

Card Number:

Issue No (Maestro only): Valid from (Maestro):

Card Security Number: Expires:

Signature:

Name Mr/Mrs/Ms ..........................................

Address ..........................................

..........................................

..........................................

.......................... Postcode ..................

Daytime Tel No ..........................................

Email ..........................................

Valid to 31/12/20

Free Print - see overleaf

**Can you help us with information about any of the Frith photographs in this book?**

We are gradually compiling an historical record for each of the photographs in the Frith archive. It is always fascinating to find out the names of the people shown in the pictures, as well as insights into the shops, buildings and other features depicted.

If you recognize anyone in the photographs in this book, or if you have information not already included in the author's caption, do let us know. We would love to hear from you, and will try to publish it in future books or articles.

**An Invitation from The Francis Frith Collection to Share Your Memories**

The 'Share Your Memories' feature of our website allows members of the public to add personal memories relating to the places featured in our photographs, or comment on others already added. Seeing a place from your past can rekindle forgotten or long held memories. Why not visit the website, find photographs of places you know well and add YOUR story for others to read and enjoy? We would love to hear from you!

**www.francisfrith.com/memories**

**Our production team**

Frith books are produced by a small dedicated team at offices near Salisbury. Most have worked with the Frith Collection for many years. All have in common one quality: they have a passion for the Frith Collection.

**Frith Books and Gifts**

We have a wide range of books and gifts available on our website utilising our photographic archive, many of which can be individually personalised.

**www.francisfrith.com**

Contains material sourced from responsibly managed forests.

FF020900